MONEY CAN BE CREATED

A Million Dollars Publication LTD

ROY SAKALA

A MILLION DOLLARS PUBLISHING COMPANY LTD

Plot No. 200/ 17, Zambezi Rd, Lusaka Zambia.

+260770401717 For International Orders +27 67 861 3824

TABLE OF CONTENTS

FOREWORD

Every day, individuals across the globe engage in activities that enable them to generate income. Ecclesiastes 10:19 underscores the undeniable truth that "money answereth all things, "emphasizing the significance of possessing wealth and why life becomes arduous without it.

Throughout history, countless people have failed to master the art of wealth creation since it extends beyond just working, providing services, or selling goods. Although these three categories are crucial for generating income, not everyone who participates in them produces the type of revenue that inspired this remarkable resource's title.

Discussing the concept of "Money Creation" entails exploring the process of generating wealth that not everyone has access to. However, it is this kind of money that sets individuals apart and elevates their status in society. Although life is a gift from God, its quality can be enhanced and improved through financial means. Money possesses purchasing power, which enables its possessor to lead an easier life and even provide aid to others if they so choose. Therefore, learning how to create wealth is a worthwhile pursuit.

The book at hand serves as an expert resource for those seeking ways and strategies on making money. It contains tried-and-tested principles presented in meticulous detail that can guide readers from scratch towards becoming successful business tycoons, depending on their personal ambition. Just as aspiring pilots take lessons from experienced aviators who possess vast knowledge about flying planes around the world, individuals looking to learn how to generate income effectively should seek guidance from experts who have successfully created wealth themselves.

Mr Roy Sakala's classic book provides excellent details on this subject matter - serving as a masterly manual book for anyone seeking practical and realistic advice on creating wealth using principles that work for people regardless of race, religion orientation or social background.

The book "Money Can Be Created "offers insightful and practical knowledge that sets it apart from other books on the same subject. It is a valuable resource for those with ambition to make money but lack understanding of the necessary steps. The book emphasizes courage and vision as essential components in the journey towards wealth creation, providing guidance not only on how to create money, but also on how to begin that journey and achieve one's dreams. Whether you are already established in business or just starting out, this book can help propel you onto Forbes' list of successful entrepreneurs. Its contents are comparable to what some people pay hundreds or even thousands of dollars for at seminars or talk shows - making it an excellent investment.

The author Roy Sakala is a businessman whom I have known for many years; he began his own entrepreneurial ventures while still pursuing academic studies during his teenage years. He believes that money is an idea which should always make sense, and has invested heavily in knowledge related to wealth creation through various means such as investing in lending companies and agriculture- becoming one of Zambia's fastest rising commercial farmers. As one of the most prominent businessmen in Zambia today. Roy is also an academician, researcher and scholar. Inspired to compile this book listing the principles that works and keeps working for him and others.

It is an indisputable fact that a great many individuals have an insatiable thirst for knowledge and information, owing to the immense significance thereof. Allow me to extend my heartfelt congratulations to you for selecting this book as your guide on how money can be created; rest assured that your quest for enlightenment will be expertly handled. As you peruse the pages of this tome at a leisurely pace, I strongly recommend that you keep a ballpoint pen and notebook close by, so as to take note of all the salient points contained therein. This invaluable resource will equip you with all the tools necessary to embark upon an ambitious journey towards wealth and prosperity - one which separates mere boys from men. Truly, money creation lies within your grasp; even as we speak there are those who are making it happen, and now it's time for you to join their ranks. However, creating wealth requires discipline: failure in this regard echoes a lack of discipline - something which is absolutely essential when striving towards financial success.

Lastly, allow me to express my sincerest congratulations to Mr Roy Sakala on having produced such a timeless masterpiece - one which has the power to transform lives in ways beyond measure! I wish him good health and much continued success in his ongoing efforts aimed at crafting impactful books whilst training others on effective strategies pertaining specifically to money management and wealth creation. All the best wishes go out not only for this particular publication but also any others he may produce in future endeavors!

Michael Zona Sakala (Poverty Eradication Program Zambia Board Chairman)

INTRODUCTION

The book "Money Can Be Created "is not merely a conventional tome, but rather an extraordinary piece of literature designed to inspire individuals who aspire for greatness. If you possess a fervent desire to become an entrepreneur, I will aid you in cultivating a sense of purpose for whatever endeavor you choose to pursue. It is important to keep in mind that the path towards achieving your goals requires unwavering determination more so than anything else. Therefore, read this book attentively as I implore you to never forget that no level of success is unattainable. Within these pages, we shall provide detailed instructions on how money can be generated.

Money serves as a universal language understood by all; however, regrettably not everyone who possesses the ability to generate money generates it. It should be noted that money simply represents value and your ideas inherently hold intrinsic worth; henceforth it is the quality rather than quantity of your concepts which determines the value of your business venture and subsequently its potential profitability. The higher the value imparted by your ideas, the greater financial gains may follow.

The Author,

Roy Sakala.

STARTUP BUSINESS PLANS/IDEAS

Comprehensive business plan entails delineating an enterprise's prospective objectives and the tactics employed to attain them, all documented in written form. Create a business blueprint that encompasses your aspirations, approaches, and intended audience.

It's important to have all your business ideas outlined in your business plan because it will help in keeping you rafting a

focused. Below are 8 steps that have been of really great help to me as I come up with business plans.

1.Develop a business plan that outlines your goals, strategies, and target market.

One of the paramount qualities that an entrepreneur must possess is the aptitude to articulate their business plans in a comprehensive manner. This can be accomplished through various mediums such as jotting down notes in a notebook, creating a PowerPoint presentation or employing any other suitable format. By doing so, it provides an insightful projection of the desired outcomes for your forthcoming enterprise.

It is crucial to delineate your objectives with utmost clarity, as having direction holds greater significance than velocity. Many individuals are rapidly progressing towards nowhere.

Ensure your strategies are authentic as they determine the success or failure of your progress. The key factor is not the type of business strategy you implement but rather how you execute it. Person X and person Y may both be selling identical products or services, yet one may generate more revenue than the other.

Finally, in the business realm, it is imperative to comprehend your target audience. Doing so will prevent you from introducing a suitable enterprise to an unsuitable market or presenting an unsuitable venture to a suitable market.

2. Conduct market research to understand your competition and identify gaps in the market.

When Sir Francis Bacon penned the phrase "knowledge itself is power" in his work, Meditationes Sacrae (1597), he likely intended to convey that possessing and disseminating knowledge serves as a fundamental basis for both one's reputation and influence, thereby granting power; all accomplishments stem from this foundation.

In your endeavor to conduct a research and comprehend your competition, it is important to note that you are not competing with individuals or their enterprises. Rather, you are entering into a competition of ideas. This entails studying and understanding the business concepts of those who have already established themselves in the market that you aspire to join. By doing so, you can identify where their ideas fall short and determine how to improve upon them, thus positioning yourself ahead of the challenging competition in the marketplace. This includes surpassing competitors' shortcomings in all areas. It is crucial to remember that what will differentiate your brand from others on the market is not solely based on selling goods or offering services but rather providing high-quality products and services while maintaining uniqueness. Strive for originality as this will attract esteemed customers and clients alike.

It is imperative to adhere to one golden rule: treat each customer and client equally regardless of size or prominence as they may hold invaluable potential for catapulting your business towards success.

3.Consider starting a business in an industry you have experience or passion in.

One of the most fatal errors that many entrepreneurs make in this era, which has maximized the potential for anyone willing to pay the price to reach the top, is venturing into businesses not because of their passion or experience but merely because it's what everyone else is doing. It's crucial to take heed and pursue your passions and interests as they significantly increase your chances of success.

Take heed, pursue your passions and interests as the likelihood of achieving success is significantly greater. This will inspire you to devote yourself unwaveringly to working towards bringing that business idea that keeps you awake at night into fruition. Failing to do so would result in inevitable failure and wasted resources.

Leveraging one's past experiences presents a unique advantage, enabling one to learn from previous missteps and blunders. Armed with this knowledge, future actions can be informed leading to enhanced outcomes in subsequent pursuits.

4.Explore innovative ideas that solve problems for customers and add value to their lives.

One of the quickest paths to achieving wealth involves identifying and addressing issues within one's community while simultaneously providing value to the general populace. Entrepreneurial problem-solving entails utilizing innovation and creative solutions in order to bridge societal, business, or technological gaps. Occasionally, personal dilemmas can translate into entrepreneurial opportunities if they are viable within the market. The entrepreneur envisions filling these gaps with innovative solutions that may require product revision or even creation from scratch. In any event, entrepreneurs approach this problem-solving process through a variety of methods.

5.Create a unique selling proposition that sets your business apart from competitors.

In order to succeed in the competitive world of business, it is essential to make your brand stand out among the rest. It is important to provide the general public with a compelling reason to choose your goods and services over those offered by your competitors. This requires a thorough understanding of your target market and their needs, as well as a clear articulation of the unique value proposition that sets your business apart.

To achieve this, you must convince your audience that your products or services are worth their time and money. This can be accomplished through effective marketing strategies and messaging that highlights the benefits and advantages of choosing your brand. Whether it is superior quality, exceptional customer service, or innovative features, you must clearly communicate what makes your business special and worthy of consideration.

Ultimately, building a successful business requires careful planning, strategic thinking, and a commitment to excellence in all aspects of operations. By focusing on what sets you apart from competitors, demonstrating value to customers, and carefully managing resources, you can position yourself for long-term success in today's dynamic marketplace.

6.Determine the resources needed to start your business, such as funding, equipment, and personnel.

Commencing a business venture necessitates resources. This is akin to a fisherman who cannot embark on his fishing expedition without carrying worms, which he will use as bait to lure the fish onto the hooks. Similarly, you must utilize what you possess in order to acquire that which you lack - this is where business capital comes into play.

It's crucial to be cognizant of the overall costs and the precise amount of funds required for your enterprise. You should also factor in equipment expenses and personnel requirements necessary for establishing your business. Furthermore, selecting an appropriate location is paramount.

Your business plan ought to have all these monetary figures correctly outlined.

7.Seek advice from experienced entrepreneurs or mentors who can provide guidance and support throughout your journey.

When embarking on a new business venture, seeking guidance from experienced individuals in the same industry is crucial for success. These mentors can offer valuable insights and advice that can prepare ordinary people for an extraordinary future. It's important to continuously evaluate and adjust your business plan as necessary, especially to adapt to changing market conditions and customer needs. By staying flexible and open-minded, you can position yourself for long-term growth and profitability. Remember that mentorship and adaptability are key ingredients in building a successful business that can withstand the challenges of today's ever-evolving marketplace.

8.Continuously evaluate and adjust your business plan as necessary to adapt to changing market conditions and customer needs.

To have a successful business, it's important to always be aware of what is happening in the market and what your customers want. This means that you need to keep an eye on any changes that happen and adjust your business plan accordingly.

For example, if there is suddenly a new competitor offering similar products or services as yours at a lower price, you may need to adjust your pricing strategy or find other ways to differentiate yourself from them.

Similarly, if you notice that your customers are asking for additional features or services that you don't currently offer, it may be necessary to update your business plan and make changes so that you can meet their needs.

By continuously evaluating and adjusting your business plan based on changing market conditions and customer needs, you can ensure that your business stays relevant and competitive over time.

At this point we have not yet started doing business, rather I have just outlined for you what you should do as you set up a business plan. We have a long day to go for you to realize what I mean when I say money can be created.

THE VISIONARY AND RESELIENT ENTREPRENEUR

The text is describing a type of entrepreneur who is both visionary and resilient. A visionary entrepreneur has the ability to see opportunities where others may not, and can come up with innovative ideas for new products or services. They are often able to anticipate changes in the market and adapt their business accordingly.

A resilient entrepreneur is someone who can bounce back from setbacks and challenges, such as economic downturns or unexpected obstacles. They have a strong sense of determination and perseverance, which allows them to keep pushing forward even when things get tough.

Together, these qualities make for a powerful combination in an entrepreneur. By being both visionary and resilient, they are able to identify new opportunities while also weathering any storms that may arise along the way. This can lead to great success in business.

For example, consider Elon Musk - he is known for his vision of transforming transportation with electric cars and space exploration through SpaceX. However, he has also faced numerous setbacks along the way including failed rocket launches and production issues with Tesla vehicles. Despite these challenges, he remains determined to achieve his goals.

Being a visionary and resilient entrepreneur is no easy feat. It requires a plethora of skills, including creativity, foresight, persistence, flexibility, and adaptability. These key traits are essential in building successful businesses over time. Creativity enables entrepreneurs to think outside the box and come up with innovative solutions to problems that may arise. Foresight allows them to anticipate future trends and stay ahead of the curve. Persistence ensures they keep pushing forward even when faced with setbacks or obstacles. Flexibility allows them to pivot and adjust their strategies as needed. And finally, adaptability enables them to thrive in ever-changing business environments. Without these traits, it can be challenging for entrepreneurs to navigate the complex world of business and achieve long-term success.

How to become a visionary and resilient entrepreneur

Becoming a visionary and resilient entrepreneur requires a combination of innate qualities and learned skills. While some individuals may possess these traits naturally, others can develop them through practice and experience.

One way to become a visionary entrepreneur is to stay informed about industry trends and emerging technologies. This allows you to identify potential opportunities before they become mainstream. Additionally, networking with other entrepreneurs and attending conferences or workshops can help you gain new perspectives and insights.

To become more resilient, it's important to cultivate a growth mindset. This means viewing setbacks as opportunities for learning and growth rather than failures. It also involves developing coping strategies for managing stress, such as exercise, meditation, or talking with a mentor.

Another key aspect of resilience is building a strong support network. This includes surrounding yourself with positive influences who can offer encouragement and advice when needed.

Ultimately, becoming a visionary and resilient entrepreneur requires commitment, hard work, and perseverance. By continuously learning, adapting, and pushing forward despite obstacles, you can achieve your goals and build a successful business that stands the test of time.

PROJECT MANAGEMENT

Project management is an integral part of any successful business venture as it involves a lot of planning, organizing, and executing tasks to achieve specific objectives within a pre-determined timeframe and budget. One of the most critical elements of project management is creating a detailed project plan that outlines all the necessary steps and resources required to complete the project successfully, along with timelines and deadlines for each task. It's also crucial to review and update this plan regularly to ensure everything stays on track.

Communication is another vital aspect of project management. Effective communication plays a significant role in ensuring that everyone involved in the project understands their roles and responsibilities, as well as any changes or updates that may arise during the course of the project. It's essential to have open lines of communication among team members so that they can report progress or issues quickly without causing delays.

In addition to having effective communication channels, it's crucial to have a system in place for monitoring progress and identifying any issues or roadblocks that may arise during the project. This allows for quick resolution of problems and helps keep the project moving forward smoothly. By staying on top of potential challenges, businesses can avoid costly delays or setbacks.

Finally, successful project management requires strong leadership skills. A good leader is capable of motivating and inspiring team members while delegating tasks effectively. They are also willing to make tough decisions when needed to ensure the success of the project.

Implementing effective project management strategies can help businesses improve efficiency, reduce costs, and increase overall success rates. Whether launching new products or services or merely looking to improve existing operations, effective project management can be instrumental in achieving goals more quickly and efficiently than ever before. With careful planning, clear communication, vigilant monitoring, strong leadership skills, businesses can achieve their goals with ease while maintaining high standards throughout every stage of their projects.

When embarking on a business project, it can be helpful to view it as a series of steps taken to execute your overall business plan. Rather than simply being a one-time event or action, a project involves careful planning, coordination, and execution to achieve specific goals and objectives. By breaking down the project into smaller tasks and milestones, you can better manage resources, stay on track with timelines and budgets, and ultimately bring your business vision to life. Whether you're launching a new product line, expanding into new markets, or implementing process improvements within your organization, approaching your project with a clear plan and attention to detail can help ensure its success. Great things are achieved by a series of small accomplishments put together.

UNDERSTANDING THE BUSINESS SYSTEMS

For any entrepreneur looking to succeed in their ventures, it is crucial to have a deep understanding of the business systems. This involves comprehending the various components of a business, including its structure, processes, and operations. By gaining an in-depth knowledge of these elements, entrepreneurs can make informed decisions that will help them achieve their goals more effectively.

One of the critical components of a business system is its structure. This refers to how the organization is organized and managed, including its hierarchy, departments, and reporting lines. Understanding this structure can help entrepreneurs identify areas where improvements can be made and ensure that everyone within the organization understands their roles and responsibilities.

Another essential aspect of business systems is the processes involved in running a successful enterprise. This includes everything from marketing and sales to production and customer service. By analyzing these processes, entrepreneurs can identify areas where they can reduce costs or improve efficiency while maintaining high standards.

Finally, understanding the operations of a business system involves knowing how it interacts with other businesses and entities in its industry or market. This includes supply chains, partnerships, and collaborations with other organizations. By understanding these relationships, entrepreneurs can identify opportunities for growth or expansion while mitigating potential risks.

Overall, building a successful enterprise requires careful analysis of all aspects of the organization's structure, processes, and operations while keeping an eye on market trends and opportunities for growth. With this knowledge in hand, entrepreneurs can make informed decisions that will help them achieve their goals more efficiently while maintaining high standards throughout every stage of their ventures. Therefore, having a thorough understanding of the business systems is essential for any entrepreneur who wants to thrive in today's competitive marketplace.

As an individual who comprehends business systems, I would like to impart my perspective on the matter. While a business system may appear as previously outlined, I delve deeper into examining how various structures within the system are interconnected and interact with one another. My focus then shifts towards devising methods of manipulating these systems to my advantage. For instance, if owning two shops generates a monthly profit of $4,000, I contemplate the possibility of owning ten such establishments where each shop yields $2,000 in profits. This line of reasoning enables me to project potential earnings from operating under such a system. Anyway a topic in this book is coming where I explain how we are going to manipulate the business systems to our advantage in details.

THE ART OF WEIGHING RISKS AGAINST LOSSES AND PROFITS.

The art of weighing risks against losses and profits is a crucial skill for any entrepreneur to possess. This involves assessing the potential risks associated with a particular business venture and determining whether the potential profits outweigh those risks.

To do this effectively, entrepreneurs must have a thorough understanding of their industry or market and be able to identify potential threats or challenges that may arise. They must also be able to analyze financial data and projections to determine the expected profitability of their venture.

Once these factors have been considered, entrepreneurs can weigh the risks against the potential profits to make an informed decision about whether to proceed with their venture. It's important not to overlook potential risks or underestimate their impact on the business, as this can lead to costly mistakes down the line.

Ultimately, successful entrepreneurs are those who are willing to take calculated risks while also being mindful of potential losses. By weighing these factors carefully and making informed decisions, they can position themselves for long-term success in today's dynamic marketplace.

Ten steps to follow when taking a risk

Taking risks is an essential part of being an entrepreneur. However, it's important to take calculated risks and weigh them against potential losses and profits. Here are ten steps to follow when taking a risk:

1. Identify the potential risks associated with your venture.

When starting a new business or project, it is important to consider the possible dangers that may arise. These risks can come in different forms such as financial loss, legal issues, safety hazards and so on. Identifying these potential risks ahead of time allows you to take necessary precautions and plan accordingly.

For example, if you are opening a restaurant, some potential risks could include food poisoning lawsuits or kitchen fires. By recognizing these threats early on, you can implement strict hygiene protocols and invest in fire safety equipment to prevent any accidents from happening.

In short, identifying the potential risks associated with your venture means analyzing all aspects of your business idea and anticipating any negative outcomes that might occur. This will help you prepare for them before they happen and minimize their impact on your success.

2. Analyze financial data and projections to determine the expected profitability of your venture.

This text is telling us to look at financial information and predictions in order to figure out how much money we can expect to make from our business idea. Essentially, it's asking us to do some research and calculations so that we can estimate whether or not our venture will be profitable (meaning we'll earn more money than we spend). This might involve looking at things like sales projections, expenses, and market trends. By analyzing this data carefully, we can get a better sense of what kind of return on investment (ROI) we might be able to expect if we decide to move forward with our business plan.

3. Consider the impact of these potential risks on your business.

The text is asking you to think about how certain risks could affect your business. These risks could be things like natural disasters, economic downturns, or changes in technology. By considering these potential risks, you can prepare for them and take steps to minimize their impact on your business. For example, if a major storm is predicted to hit your area, you might make sure that all of your important data is backed up and stored in a safe place so that it doesn't get lost or damaged during the storm. Or if there's a new competitor entering the market who offers similar products or services as yours at lower prices, you might consider adjusting your pricing strategy or finding ways to differentiate yourself from the competition. Overall, by being aware of potential risks and taking proactive measures to address them, you can help ensure the long-term success of your business.

4. Evaluate the likelihood of each risk occurring.

When evaluating risks, it is important to consider how likely each risk is to actually happen. This means examining the probability or chance of each risk occurring. For example, if you are planning an outdoor event and one of the potential risks is rain, you would want to evaluate how likely it is that it will rain on the day of your event.

By assessing the likelihood of each risk, you can prioritize which risks need more attention and resources in order to mitigate or prevent them from happening. If a particular risk has a high likelihood of occurring, then it may require more preparation and planning than a lower-risk scenario.

Overall, evaluating the likelihood of each risk helps you make informed decisions about how best to manage those risks and ensure that your project or event runs smoothly with minimal disruption.

5. Determine the potential losses associated with each risk.

When we talk about risk, it means that there is a possibility of something bad happening. For example, if you are planning to go on a trip, the risk could be losing your luggage or getting sick while traveling. To understand how much harm these risks can cause us, we need to determine their potential losses.

This means identifying what kind of damage each risk could do and estimating how much it would cost us in terms of money or other resources. For instance, if our risk is losing our luggage during travel, we must consider the value of all items inside the bag and estimate how expensive it would be to replace them.

By determining potential losses associated with each risk beforehand, we can prepare ourselves better for any situation that might occur. This will help us take necessary precautions and minimize damages as much as possible.

6.Weigh the potential losses against the expected profits.

This text is advising you to consider the possible negative outcomes or risks of a decision alongside the anticipated gains or benefits. Essentially, it's important to evaluate whether the potential losses outweigh the expected profits before making a choice. For example, if you're thinking about investing in a new business venture, you should carefully assess the potential risks and costs involved versus what you hope to gain from this investment. By weighing these factors against each other, you can make an informed decision that minimizes your chances of experiencing significant financial losses.

7. Consider alternative options that may be less risky but still profitable.

This text is suggesting that when making a decision, it's important to think about other options that may not be as risky but can still make money. For example, if you're thinking about investing in stocks and are worried about the risk of losing your money, you could consider putting your money into bonds instead. While bonds may not have as high of a potential return on investment as stocks do, they also come with less risk.

In simpler terms if you want to venture into keeping pigs in a piggery you would instead venture in chicken poultry business, which is much cheaper to start but highly profitable if done correctly.

Similarly, if you're considering starting a new business venture but are concerned about the risks involved, you might explore alternative business models or strategies that could potentially yield profits without taking on as much financial risk.

The idea behind this text is to encourage people to think creatively and explore different options before making decisions. By doing so, individuals can increase their chances of success while minimizing potential losses or negative consequences.

8.Seek advice from experienced entrepreneurs or mentors who can provide guidance and support throughout your journey.

If you're starting a business or embarking on an entrepreneurial journey, it can be really helpful to have someone who has been there before to guide and support you. That's where experienced entrepreneurs or mentors come in! These are people who have already gone through the ups and downs of starting and growing a business, and they're willing to share their knowledge with others.

By seeking advice from these experts, you can learn from their mistakes, get tips on how to navigate challenges, and gain insights into what works (and what doesn't) when it comes to building a successful company. They can also provide emotional support when things get tough, which is especially important since entrepreneurship can be a lonely road at times.

So if you're thinking about starting your own business or taking your current venture to the next level, don't go it alone! Reach out to experienced entrepreneurs or mentors for guidance and support along the way.

9. Continuously evaluate and adjust your plan as necessary to adapt to changing market conditions and customer needs.

This text is telling us that it's important to always be checking and changing our plans in response to changes in the market or what customers want. So, if you have a plan for your business or project, but then something happens like a new competitor comes into the market or customers start wanting something different from what you offer, you need to adjust your plan accordingly. This means keeping an eye on what's happening around you and being flexible enough to change course when necessary. It can help keep your business successful and make sure you're meeting the needs of your customers as they evolve over time.

10.Be willing to make tough decisions when needed to ensure the success of your venture.

To ensure that your business or project succeeds, you need to be prepared to make difficult decisions. Sometimes these choices may not be easy or popular, but they are necessary for the greater good of your venture. For example, if one of your employees is not performing well and is negatively impacting the team's productivity, you may have to make the tough decision to let them go in order to maintain a successful work environment. Making these kinds of tough calls can be challenging, but ultimately it will help move your venture forward towards success.

By following these steps, entrepreneurs can take calculated risks while also being mindful of potential losses and ensuring long-term success in today's dynamic marketplace. Remember, taking risks is necessary for growth, but it's crucial to do so in a way that minimizes potential harm while maximizing potential rewards.

THE GREATEST BUSINESS MAN

If you have managed to read this far into my book, it indicates that you are determined to become the next great business magnate. Allow me to share some secrets with you.

First and foremost, I want you to understand that the most successful business people did not begin with vast amounts of capital. All great accomplishments start out small. The amount of money at your disposal does not matter; I have observed individuals who started out with a large sum but could not sustain their enterprise over time, while others with limited resources proceeded to achieve remarkable success in the world of commerce.

To become an exceptional entrepreneur, eliminate procrastination from your life. Sometimes all it takes is for you to create opportunities for yourself instead of waiting around for what eludes your understanding. You must simply take action because nothing ever happens on its own accord in life - if there is something that you desire, then make it happen! Whatever it is that you are waiting for is also waiting patiently for your initiative.

Failure constitutes an integral part of the process involved in traversing the path towards becoming a successful business person; believe me when I say that during this journey, depression, rejection and disappointment will be prevalent feelings experienced by many entrepreneurs. However, do not allow any obstacle or setback encountered along the way break down your spirit; rather use them as motivation and encouragement to persevere through whatever circumstances may arise.

If someone were to tell you that establishing a thriving company was easy or akin to lying on a bed of roses while amassing wealth quickly and easily - they would be regarded as one of history's greatest liars! It should be noted however that failures and challenges will be frequent occurrences throughout this endeavour.

"It doesn't matter how many times you get knocked down. All that matters is you get up one more time than you were knocked down."-Roy T.Bennett.

Try again after failure but never stop trying altogether!

A truly outstanding businessman/woman should possess a strong heart or spirit- never giving up on what he/she believes in no matter how long it takes- patience is key!

Do not let fear prevent greatness from being achieved; everything worth achieving lies just beyond our fears.

At all costs avoid distractions young man/young woman/dear sir/madam...develop good spending habits: do NOT buy anything unplanned unless absolutely necessary; some people tend go overboard upon receiving funds such as buying dog food despite having no pet dog whatsoever among other things...good personal spending habits save us from unnecessary financial constraints/risk-taking so please always exercise caution! Lastly- Do NOT feel discouraged because starting a lucrative venture/business endeavor remains possible even today!

Below is an extract inspirational story please note that this book is not about inspirational stories it's about how money can be created however just to enlighten you from examples of how certain great people did it from nothing to the top should really leave you with no choice but starting up your own business. I'll share few stories in this book.

Let's briefly look into the story KFC and it's founder.

Inspiring life story of KFC's Colonel Sanders.

Sanders was born in 1890 in Henryville, IN. When he was six years old, his father passed away leaving Sanders to cook and care for his siblings. In seventh grade, he dropped out of school and left home to go work as a farmhand. Already turning into a tough cookie.

At 16, he faked his age to enlist in the United States army. After being honorably discharged a year later, he got hired by the railway as a laborer. However, he got fired for fighting with a coworker. While he worked for the railway, he studied law--until he ruined his legal career by getting into another fight. Sanders was forced to move back in with his mom and get a job selling life insurance. And guess what? He got fired for insubordination. But this guy wouldn't give up.

In 1920, he founded a ferry boat company. Later, he tried cashing in his ferry boat business to create a lamp manufacturing company only to find out that another company already sold a better version of his lamp. Poor guy couldn't catch a break.

It wasn't until age 40 that he began selling chicken dishes in a service station. As he began to advertise his food, an argument with a competitor resulted in a deadly shootout. Four years later, he bought a motel which burned to the ground along with his restaurant. Yet this determined man rebuilt and ran a new motel until World War II forced him to close it down.

Following the war, he tried to franchise his restaurant. His recipe was rejected 1,009 times before anyone accepted it. Sander's "secret recipe" was coined "Kentucky Fried Chicken", and quickly became a hit. However, the booming restaurant was crippled when an interstate opened nearby so Sanders sold it and pursued his dream of spreading KFC franchises & hiring KFC workers all across the country.

After years of failures and misfortunes, Sanders finally hit it big. KFC expanded internationally and he sold the company for two million dollars ($15.3 million today). Even today, Sanders remains central in KFC's branding and his face still appears in their logo. His goatee, white suit and western string tie continue to symbolize delicious country fried chicken all over the world.

At age 90, Sanders passed away from pneumonia. At that time, there were around 6,000 KFC locations in 48 countries. By 2013, there were an estimated 18,000 KFC locations in 118 countries. WOW.

If you're overwhelmed by rejection or discouraged by setbacks, remember the story of Colonel Harland Sanders. Fired from multiple jobs, ruined his legal career, was set back by the Great Depression, fires and World War II, yet still created one of the largest fast food chains in the world. Sanders wouldn't let anything or anyone defeat him. We should all be more like Colonel Sanders. Moreover he did not start with great capital you see.

In this context I won' define the greatest business man/woman as the richest of them all no but the one who creates a large establishment despite having small resources and suffering so many setbacks. You and I can become the next Colonel sanders.

SETTING UP YOU OWN BUSINESS SYSTEMS

At this point I'll take it like you already understand the business systems because we already discussed it in the topic Understanding the business systems. Let's continue on the story which we had cut short. As I was explaining, For instance, if owning two shops generates a monthly profit of $4,000, I contemplate the possibility of owning ten such establishments where each shop yields $2,000 in profits. This line of reasoning enables me to project potential earnings from operating under such a system.

Let's take a relatable example, where I own two hardware and automotive parts shops. These stores sell various household hardware products like fasteners, building materials, hand tools, power tools, keys, locks, hinges, chains, plumbing supplies, electrical supplies along with cleaning products and housewares to consumers for their home or business needs. Additionally in both my shops we offer services such as installation of the purchased items. In the same shops we also deal with automotive spare parts and provide customers with the option to purchase parts as well as fixing them through our workshop.

Moving forward to profits generated from these stores; owning two such outlets generates me a profit of $4,000 monthly ($2,000 per shop). If I were to expand this business by opening eight more branches in different high traffic locations within big cities that have similar demand levels then my total number of shops would be ten. With every store generating $2,000 in profit each month it is easy to calculate that I would earn approximately $20,000 per month from all ten stores combined.

This scenario is just one example of how manipulating the business system can work towards your advantage irrespective of whether you are running a bakery , restaurant , hotel , grocery store (either retail or wholesale) boutique or even poultry farms/fish ponds, transportation etc . It's not always about working hard but rather working smart.

By smartly setting up systems which will work for you while earning money even when asleep!

Try this you'll thank me later.

PAY THE PRICE

A trade-off occurs when one gives up something desired in exchange for another desired item. When goods are limited, consumers must choose from a finite selection of products and therefore, to consume a specific good, they must make a trade-off by giving up the opportunity to obtain another good. In simpler terms, if someone wants to purchase the latest Rolls Royce that costs $500,000, they must be willing to let go of that exact amount of money in order to possess the car.

To achieve success as an entrepreneur requires making sacrifices and working hard towards becoming proficient in business. This includes investing time and resources into gaining extensive knowledge about one's industry or market and honing relevant skills to become an expert in their field. A strong work ethic is vital for paying this price which encompasses putting in long hours and enduring sleepless nights while staying focused on objectives even amidst distractions or setbacks.

Moreover, continuous learning and self-improvement are crucial aspects of succeeding as an entrepreneur which may involve attending seminars or workshops along with reading books/articles about entrepreneurship or seeking guidance from experienced mentors who can offer support throughout one's journey.

Taking calculated risks is also pivotal since entrepreneurs should be prepared for potential losses but still have the willingness to take chances towards achieving success; it means pursuing opportunities outside their comfort zone even if they seem daunting at first glance.

Ultimately, attaining greatness as an entrepreneur demands discipline combined with hard work alongside risk-taking tendencies and perseverance. By dedicating oneself entirely towards this pursuit without giving up on aspirations even during challenging times will lead them towards achieving greatness within today's dynamic marketplace.

ASSETS AND LIABILITIES

An asset is something valuable that you own, like money or property, and can bring you benefits in the future. It can help you make money, save money, or improve your sales. Assets can be grouped into various categories, such as current assets (like cash or securities), fixed assets (like buildings or machinery), financial assets (like bonds or stocks), or intangible assets (like patents or copyrights).

Personal assets include things like a home, land, financial investments, jewelry, artwork, or money in your bank account. Business assets can include vehicles, buildings, machinery, equipment, cash, or money owed to the business.

On the other hand, a liability is something that you owe to someone else. It can also represent legal or regulatory obligations or risks. Examples of liabilities are loans, unpaid bills, mortgages, deferred revenues, bonds, warranties, or expenses that have accrued.

To simplify, an asset brings in money, while a liability takes money away from you. It is generally better to focus on acquiring assets rather than spending money on liabilities. Let's look at an example:

Imagine two people, Person A and Person B, both starting with $50,000.

Person A ventures into real estate business.

Person A decides to invest their money by building five mini apartments to rent out. Each month, Person A earns $5,000 from these rentals, making $25,000 per month in total. Even if Person A loses their job, it won't be a problem because they have these assets generating income. In just two months, Person A can recover their initial investment. They can even expand their apartment business to create a system that works for them without needing to actively work.

On the other hand, Person B spends their money on buying a car and an expensive iPhone. The car requires monthly expenses like fuel and maintenance costs, while the iPhone needs monthly internet bills. Person B's expenses keep taking money away, leaving them unable to afford gas, car servicing, or internet bills.

In conclusion, it's important to prioritize acquiring assets over spending on liabilities. While liabilities may seem appealing, it's pointless to have luxury items if you end up with nothing in your bank account. Sacrificing luxury in the present for future assets is a wise approach.

Assets are anything your business owns that can generate cash in the future, whether through sales, business operations, or increasing the value of your business. They can be quickly converted into money (liquid assets) or take longer to generate cash (low liquidity assets). Besides cash and financial investments, assets can include tools, equipment, or intellectual property.

Liabilities represent your financial obligations to others, such as loans, taxes, or insurance payments. Keeping track of liabilities is important to ensure you have enough funds to pay them off on time.

In accounting, assets and liabilities are listed in a balance sheet, which shows your business's financial health. The net worth or owner's equity of your business is determined by subtracting your total liabilities from your total assets. To increase the worth of your business, you need to have more assets than liabilities.

To manage your cash effectively in terms of assets and liabilities, consider a three-step approach called the tri-systematic matrix:

- Plan A: Invest your money in assets that passively generate income.

- Plan B: Use the money earned from Plan A to increase your assets, earning even more income.

- Plan C: Spend some of the money from Plan A on liabilities, if needed.

Remember, this is a simplified explanation of assets and liabilities, and there are many more aspects to consider.

THE TRUTH ABOUT SAVING MONEY

Saving money is a fundamental financial practice that involves allocating a portion of your earnings for future use. However, it's crucial to comprehend the appropriate time and method to save effectively.

What does saving money entail? It entails setting aside a fraction of your income or earnings regularly instead of spending everything. The aim is to create a financial cushion, achieve monetary objectives, or have resources accessible for emergencies.

When should you save and when shouldn't you? It's recommended to save money when you have surplus income beyond immediate needs and expenses. In times of financial crisis or significant debt, it may be wiser to temporarily halt regular savings and focus on resolving the pressing issues. Saving can also be postponed briefly if there are urgent expenses or obligations that require immediate attention.

How long should you save and how long shouldn't you? The duration of savings hinges on individual fiscal goals and circumstances. Short-term goals such as an emergency fund ought to be accomplished within months up to one year. Long-term objectives like retirement or buying property require consistent saving over numerous years or even decades. Striking a balance between saving for the future while enjoying present pleasures is vital; occasional indulgences are acceptable as long as they don't impede overall financial goals.

Can someone become wealthy by just saving money? Saving alone may not guarantee becoming affluent since wealth accumulation typically involves other strategies such as investing, generating passive income, and making wise financial decisions. Nonetheless, disciplined saving over time can establish a robust foundation for wealth accumulation while providing necessary resources for pursuing investment opportunities.

Saving from salary vs passive income: Saving from earned income (salary) is common & reliable because it involves regular contributions; however relying solely on salary savings may take longer unless one has high earnings or saves substantially more than usual percentages per month/year etc.. Passive-income generated by assets like real estate/businesses could accelerate wealth accumulation significantly - especially when reinvested intelligently furthering returns!

In conclusion: Saving money is valuable in creating stability & achieving long term fiscal ambitions but must strike balance with other methods maximizing potential.

HOW TO WORK WITH THE GOVERNMENT AS AN ENTREPRENEUR

- Collaborating with the government can provide unique opportunities for entrepreneurs to grow their businesses.

- To effectively work with the government, entrepreneurs should follow proper channels for registration, fulfill tax obligations, explore service and supply opportunities, seek legal assistance, and develop negotiation skills.

1. Registering Your Company:

- Follow the appropriate legal procedures to register your company or business as required by the government.

- Research and understand the registration requirements, which may include obtaining business licenses, permits, and certifications.

2. Paying Taxes:

- Comply with tax regulations and pay taxes to the relevant revenue authorities.

- Maintain accurate financial records to ensure proper tax reporting and transparency.

3. Explore Service Offerings to Government:

- Identify areas where your business can provide services to government entities based on their needs and requirements.

- Stay informed about government tenders, contracts, and procurement opportunities relevant to your industry.

4. Supplying Goods to the Government:

- Determine if your business can supply goods or products to government agencies.

- Keep track of government procurement processes and bid for contracts when suitable opportunities arise.

5. Engage a Business Lawyer:

- Consider working with a business lawyer who specializes in government contracts and regulations.

- Seek legal advice to ensure compliance with laws, understand contract terms, and protect your business interests.

6. Develop Negotiation Skills:

- Enhance your negotiation skills to effectively communicate and collaborate with government representatives.

- Understand government procurement procedures and be prepared to negotiate terms and pricing.

Conclusion:

- Working with the government as an entrepreneur requires following the proper channels for registration and fulfilling tax obligations.

- Explore opportunities to offer services or supply goods to government entities within your industry.

- Engage a business lawyer for legal guidance and develop negotiation skills to navigate government contracts successfully.

- Remember to stay updated on government policies and regulations to ensure compliance and maximize potential collaboration opportunities.

THE ROLE OF BANKS IN YOUR BUSINESS JOURNEY

Commercial banks are financial institutions that provide a diverse range of services to both individuals and business enterprises. Specifically, for businesses, commercial banks offer an array of services that can assist in managing finances and supporting business operations. Some vital services offered by commercial banks to businesses include:

1. Business accounts: Commercial banks provide specific types of accounts tailored to the needs of businesses, enabling them to handle and keep track of their financial transactions efficiently.

2. Loans and credit facilities: Commercial banks offer financial support through loans and credit facilities that can be used for various operational requirements such as business expansion, working capital, capital investment, among others.

3. Payment processing: Commercial banks facilitate efficient payment processing through merchant accounts, payment gateways, point-of-sale systems facilitating various payment methods like debit cards, credit cards online payments etc.

4. Transaction management: Banks offer effective tools like online banking platforms mobile banking apps electronic fund transfers secure transaction platforms etc., which help manage and track business transactions effectively.

5. Cash management: To ensure effective cash flow handling at all times; commercial banks provide cash management solutions including account reconciliation cash pooling cash forecasting &optimization among other things

6.Treasury Services : Banks also extend treasury management solutions designed specifically to help businesses manage their investments risks liquidity foreign exchange related issues . This includes advisory on risk management as well as investment decisions

7.Trade finance - International trade is facilitated with letters of credit , import/export financing , trade documentation services provided by most commercial bank

8.Business-specific services - Many commercial bank offers specialized service catering specifically to different type industries such as payroll management supply chain financing insurance policies customized financial plans etc

Overall these aforementioned features make it possible for a wide range of companies from small start-ups all the way up multinational corporations alike rely on this sector for efficient handling of finances leading towards growth opportunities.

Advantages Associated with Using Commercial Banks:

- Financial support via loans or credit facilities
- Efficient payment processing &transaction tracking
- Availability specialized business banking options
- Establishment Business Credit History/Credibility

Disadvantages Associated with using Commercial Bank :

- High Service Charges/Fees
- Complex Bureaucracy/Lengthy Processes

Criteria For Identifying Good/Bad Commercial Banks :Good Ones :
-Ease Of Access/Technological Capabilities.-Customer Service /Availability Of Business-Specific Services .-Low Interest Rates/Charges/Fees .

Bad Ones:-High Fees And Charges.-Poor Customer Feedback.-Unappealing Interest Rates/Limited Ability To Cater To Specific Business Needs.

Utilizing Savings Accounts:-Benefits Of Having A Separate Savings Account For Your Business Funds-Funds Set Aside For Future Emergencies/Growth Opportunities-Maximizing Earnings While Maintaining Liquidity

Ensuring Systematic Payments Through Company Bank Account:-Paying Employees Via The Company's Bank Account Ensures Transparency/Accuracy In Payroll Management .-Automated Payment/Payroll Systems Help Streamline Operations .

The Importance Of Hiring Experienced Accountants:-The Benefits Of Having Competent Professionals Manage Your Financial Records-Guaranteeing Compliance With Tax Requirements And Financial Regulations-Provide Strategic Financial Advice And Planning For Sustainable Growth .

STUDYING YOUR BUSINESS INDUSTRY

A Comprehensive Guide for Entrepreneurs.

Market Analysis:

- Conducting comprehensive market research to identify target customers, determine market size and potential demand.
- Analyzing industry trends, growth projections, and competition to gain valuable insights.
- Understanding consumer needs, preferences, and behaviors through in-depth analysis.

Competitive Landscape:

- Identifying both direct and indirect competitors within the marketplace.
- Evaluating competitor strengths, weaknesses, strategies, and market positioning thoroughly.
- Understanding competitive advantages that can be leveraged to differentiate your business from others.

Industry Regulations and Compliance:

- Researching industry-specific regulations comprehensively including licenses, permits as well as certifications required by the sector of operation.
- Complying with legal standards while also maintaining ethical practices during business operations.
- Staying up-to-date on any changes in regulations or industry standards that may arise over time.

Customer Segmentation:

- Identifying customer segments based on demographics such as age groupings or psychographics like interests or behavior patterns.
- Gaining an understanding of customer pain points so that you can tailor products/services accordingly.
- Creating tailored marketing strategies designed specifically for each segment.

Value Proposition:

- Articulating a unique value proposition that sets your business apart from its competitors.
- Communicating how your products or services solve customer problems or fulfill their needs effectively.
- Recognizing the competitive advantages inherent within your business model so you can leverage them successfully.

Industry Networks &Associations:

- Joining relevant networks/associations/trade organizations associated with one's particular niche/industry.
- Building meaningful relationships with other professionals within the field; suppliers/vendors/partners etc.
- Accessing crucial updates/opportunities through effective networking efforts.

Technology & Innovation:
– Assessing emerging technologies/trends likely to impact one's industry.

– Embracing technology advancements designed for improving internal processes/customer experiences thereby driving innovation forward.
– Evaluating how disruptive technologies could potentially affect one's existing business model.

Financial Considerations:
– Understanding the financial landscape of one's specific industry e.g revenue models/profit margins.
– Analyzing cost structures/pricing strategies/financial risks associated with operating a given enterprise.
– Planning/budgeting strategically towards long term sustainability/growth prospects.

Industry Challenges &Opportunities:
– Identifying major challenges/risk factors affecting current/future performance metrics.
– Developing workable solutions/mitigation plans aimed at optimizing opportunities/enhancing overall competitiveness.
– Keeping abreast of news/market disruptions/emerging trends in order to maintain an edge over rivals.

Continuous Learning & Adaptation:
– Acknowledging ongoing learning requirements whilst staying updated about latest technological breakthroughs.
– Embracing a mindset geared towards continuous improvement/adaptation.
– Being open-minded when it comes feedback/customer insights/inherent shifts taking place within various industries.

THE TRUTH ABOUT GAMBLING

GAMBLING is defined as the betting or staking of something of value, with consciousness of risk and hope of gain, on the outcome of a game, a contest, or an uncertain event whose result may be determined by chance or accident or have an unexpected result by reason of the bettor's miscalculation.

Gambling can have significant consequences on business people, impacting both their personal and professional lives. It is important to recognize and understand the potential negative effects associated with gambling:

1. Financial Consequences: Excessive gambling can lead to significant financial losses, potentially jeopardizing personal and business finances. This could result in severe debt, bankruptcy, or the depletion of funds needed for business operations and growth.

2. Time and Productivity: Engaging in gambling activities can be time-consuming and divert focus away from important business responsibilities. The excessive time spent on gambling can lead to decreased productivity, missed deadlines, and compromised business performance.

3. Mental and Emotional Well-being: Gambling addiction can have negative psychological impacts, including heightened stress levels, anxiety, and depression. These mental health issues can impact decision-making abilities, judgment, and overall mental well-being, potentially affecting business relationships and leadership capabilities.

4. Professional Reputational Risks: Problematic gambling behavior can damage an individual's professional reputation. Financial irresponsibility or ethical concerns related to gambling can lead to a loss of trust among colleagues, partners, and clients, potentially impacting business relationships and opportunities.

5. Legal and Regulatory Considerations: Gambling activities may intersect with legal and regulatory requirements, especially in industries where conflicts of interest and insider trading concerns are prevalent. Violating professional

standards, codes of conduct, or engaging in illegal gambling practices could have severe consequences, including legal penalties and the loss of professional licenses or certifications.

Recognizing the potential consequences of gambling, it is important for business people to practice responsible gambling habits, set limits, and prioritize personal well-being. Seeking professional help and support if gambling becomes problematic or addictive is crucial in mitigating potential harm and preserving both personal and business interests.

I'm not disagreeing sometimes people make millions off gambling if lucky but I want you to know that the chances of you succeeding in gambling are minimal.

Understand that the gambling systems where not designed to enrich the customers or clients but the business owners. So I Roy Sakala caution you not to engage in any form of gambling if you're a business oriented person.

GET SOME INSPIRATION

At present, allow me to share a tale related to me by my beloved mother, Ms. Mary Chisopa in 2019 when she observed my grand aspirations of becoming a businessman. She noted how I commenced my business during senior secondary school from 2016 to 2018 in Kasama, Zambia selling lollipops and snacks during break time at school.

Without further delay, let us delve into this real-life story quickly.

Several years ago, in the year 1975 while my mother was studying in grade seven, she stumbled upon a book entitled "Grade Seven Learner's Book."This book contained an authentic life account of a young man named Wesley.

Wesley was an ambitious lad whose ultimate aim was to establish a business and earn substantial profits. Unfortunately, his family members ridiculed him for his entrepreneurial vision and dismissed it as mere impractical dreams that he needed to abandon and come back down to earth.

His usual job involved washing cars as means of raising capital for his business venture. Although Wesley resided in the Chawama compound of Lusaka Zambia, he traveled daily all the way to the town center solely for car-washing duties.

One day while on duty cleaning vehicles downtown with his friend who wore an attractive tie-and-dye vest dotted with vibrant colors; Wesley admired its appearance and asked where he had obtained such fantastic attire. His friend explained that there is a woman named Mrs. Kazunga located at Chaisa compound within Lusaka who makes these trendy designs on vests besides other clothing items too! If you are interested I can take you there, "said his enthusiastic friend!

Ecstatic about this opportunity presented before him without wasting any more time; Wesley agreed instantly! The following day accompanied by his buddy they went straightaway towards Chaisa Compound within Lusaka where Mrs Kazunga lived!

Using all the money earned from car washing downtown so far; Wesley purchased four tie-and-dye vests immediately upon arrival at her place then proceeded promptly back towards Lusaka town-center where he sold everything off earning extraordinary profits since people adored wearing clothes designed like those trendy tie-and-die outfits which were very fashionable during that period around the mid-1970s era!

The next day spurred by success; Wesley ordered ten more customized vests when returning again towards town which sold out rapidly within minutes prompting him continuously repeating this process gradually increasing production volume until demand skyrocketed beyond control necessitating seeking help from Mrs.Kazunga herself requesting training lessons on how-to-make-tie-and-dye-shirts-of-his-design-branded-labels due-to overwhelming market demand!

After acquiring sufficient expertise himself making these products using raw materials sourced locally plus hiring several employees alongside opening up a factory and branches throughout various locations particularly inside-town-centers across Zambia supplying custom-made Tie-&-Dye Vests &Shirts became immensely successful turning into one among leading suppliers countrywide amassing vast fortunes after just one year succeeding beyond imagination even transforming lives of previously impoverished family members joining them together under one roof living lavishly inside newly constructed mansion built courtesy wealth amassed over-time through sheer hard-work coupled with persistence despite discouragement earlier received initially from close relatives regarding initial plans launched as outlined above proving ultimately their worthiness indeed along-with viability too!!

It's evident sometimes all we require is vision fueled via ambition strengthened via strong desire propelled forward by opportunities meeting preparedness defined commonly as luck!! Therefore always remain ready whenever opportunities arise not caught unaware or unprepared instead stay alert ever-ready always dreaming big just-like-Wesley never allowing mockery deter progress made thus far!!!

Mark Zuckerberg once famously stated: "No-one does when they begin ideas don't come out fully formed they only become clear as you work on them. You just have to get started!"

Dreaming remains free but hustle costs separately however learning valuable lessons taught herein today hopefully inspires greater drive determination pushing forward against-all-odds prevailing ultimately achieving remarkable outcomes similar-to Wesley's legendary exploits inspiring millions worldwide!!!

At present Zambia has a vibrant entrepreneurial ecosystem, with many successful business people who have made significant contributions to the country's economy. Here are some examples of successful business people in Zambia:

1. **Byenda Nkwanda**: At just 21 years old, Byenda is the CEO of Golden Traib, a fashion label that she founded herself. She was selected for the Tony Elumelu Foundation Entrepreneurship Programme in 2015 and received seed capital to grow her business.

2. **Chilufya Mutale**: Chilufya is the founder of Premier Credit, a microfinance institution that provides loans to small businesses and individuals in Zambia. The company has been instrumental in providing financial support to many entrepreneurs who would otherwise not have access to credit facilities [3].

3. **Evelyn Kaingu**: Evelyn is the co-founder of Lupiya, a fintech startup that provides digital financial services to underserved communities in Zambia. The company's mobile app allows users to access loans, savings accounts, and other financial services without having to visit a bank branch [3].

4. **Chiinga Musonda**: Chiinga is the founder of Savanna Premium Chocolate, a chocolate manufacturing company that produces high-quality chocolate using locally sourced cocoa beans. The company's products are sold both locally and internationally [3].

5. **Monica Musonda**: Monica is the founder of Java Foods, a food processing company that produces nutritious food products from locally sourced ingredients. The company's flagship product is eeZee Instant Noodles, which is made from cassava flour and has become a popular snack among Zambians [3].

These are just a few examples of successful business people in Zambia who have made significant contributions to the country's economy.

FIND A BUSINESS MENTOR

Finding a business mentor can be an invaluable resource for entrepreneurs looking to grow their businesses. A mentor is someone who has experience in your industry or field and can offer guidance, advice, and support throughout your journey.

Here are some steps to follow when finding a business mentor:

1. Identify what you need help with: Determine the areas where you need guidance or support, whether it's developing a business plan, marketing strategy, or financial management.
2. Research potential mentors: Look for individuals who have experience in your industry or field and have achieved success in their own businesses. You can find potential mentors through professional networks, online resources, or personal referrals.
3. Reach out to potential mentors: Once you've identified potential mentors, reach out to them and express your interest in learning from them. Be respectful of their time and ask if they would be willing to meet with you for a conversation or mentorship session.
4. Establish expectations: Clarify what you hope to gain from the mentorship relationship and establish clear expectations for communication and meetings.
5. Be open to feedback: Mentors can provide valuable feedback that may challenge your assumptions or beliefs about your business. Be open-minded and willing to consider different perspectives.
6. Show gratitude: Remember that mentoring is a voluntary act of generosity on the part of the mentor. Show appreciation for their time and expertise by thanking them regularly and acknowledging their contributions to your success.

Overall, finding a business mentor can help entrepreneurs navigate the challenges of starting and growing a successful enterprise while providing valuable insights into industry trends, best practices, and strategies for success. By seeking guidance from experienced professionals, entrepreneurs can increase their chances of achieving long-term success in today's dynamic marketplace.

By the way I'm available for business mentorship, if you're interested in having me as your business mentor you can contact me with via email through the contact details I've put on my book. It doesn't matter where you are distance is not a barrier.

DIVERSIFY YOUR BUSINESS INTO VARIOUS SECTORS OF THE ECONOMY

Diversifying your business into various sectors of the economy can help mitigate risks and increase opportunities for growth. By expanding into new markets or industries, businesses can tap into new customer bases, access different distribution channels, and leverage their existing resources and capabilities to create new revenue streams.

Here are some steps to follow when diversifying your business:

1. Identify potential opportunities: Research different industries or markets that align with your core competencies or offer complementary products or services. Look for areas where demand is growing or where there is untapped potential.
2. Assess risks and benefits: Evaluate the potential risks and benefits associated with entering a new market or industry. Consider factors such as competition, regulatory requirements, supply chain logistics, and financial considerations.
3. Develop a strategy: Create a strategic plan that outlines how you will enter the new market or industry, including marketing strategies, operational plans, and financial projections.
4. Allocate resources: Determine how much capital and other resources you will need to invest in order to successfully enter the new market or industry.
5. Build partnerships: Consider forming partnerships with other businesses in the target market or industry to gain access to their networks and expertise.
6. Monitor progress: Regularly monitor your progress towards achieving your diversification goals and adjust your strategy as needed based on performance metrics.

Overall, diversifying your business can be a smart move for long-term growth and sustainability. By expanding into new markets or industries while leveraging existing strengths, businesses can create multiple revenue streams while mitigating risks associated with relying on a single product or service line.

Don't put all your eggs in one basket because you might end up losing everything. Try doing something different.

Don't limit yourself to only one type of business. You might find out you can also do better in other businesses and do exploits.

UNDERSTAND YOUR COUNTRY'S ECONOMY

To succeed in business it also requires you to realize how the structures of your country's economy, this is in line with understanding the laws of supply and demand.

The laws of supply and demand are basic concepts in economics that describe how the price and quantity of a good or service are determined in a market. The law of demand states that when the price of a good or service increases, the quantity demanded by buyers decreases, and vice versa. The law of supply states that when the price of a good or service increases, the quantity supplied by sellers increases, and vice versa. These two laws can be represented by downward-sloping and upward-sloping curves on a graph, respectively[1].

The interaction between the demand and supply curves determines the equilibrium price and quantity in the market. The equilibrium price is the price at which the quantity demanded equals the quantity supplied. The equilibrium quantity is the amount of the good or service that is bought and sold at the equilibrium price. When the market is in equilibrium, there is no excess demand or excess supply, and both buyers and sellers are satisfied[1].

However, the market can be affected by various factors that shift the demand or supply curves, such as changes in income, preferences, technology, taxes, subsidies, etc. When the demand curve shifts, it causes a change in both the equilibrium price and quantity. For example, if there is an increase in demand for a good or service, the demand curve shifts to the right, resulting in a higher equilibrium price and quantity. This means that buyers are willing to pay more and buy more of the good or service at any given price.

Similarly, when the supply curve shifts, it causes a change in both the equilibrium price and quantity. For example, if there is an increase in supply of a good or service, the supply curve shifts to the right, resulting in a lower equilibrium price and quantity. This means that sellers are willing to accept less and sell more of the good or service at any given price[2].

The law of supply and demand can be applied to any type of good or service in any country's economy. It helps to explain how prices are determined by the forces of demand and supply, and how they respond to changes in market conditions. It also helps to analyze the effects of government policies, such as taxes or subsidies, on the market outcomes[3]. The law of supply and demand is one of the most fundamental concepts in economics and is widely used in various fields of study.

It's important to learn about the laws of supply and demand and how they affect the economy and business.

The laws of supply and demand are two fundamental economic principles that describe how the price of a good or service is determined by the interaction of its supply and demand in a market. Supply is the amount of a good or service that producers are willing and able to offer for sale at a given price. Demand is the amount of a good or service that consumers are willing and able to buy at a given price.

The laws of supply and demand state that:

- When supply is greater than demand, the price tends to fall.

- When demand is greater than supply, the price tends to rise.

- When supply and demand are equal, the price tends to stay the same.

These laws can be illustrated by using supply and demand curves, which show the relationship between price and quantity for a given good or service. The point where the supply and demand curves intersect is called the equilibrium point, which represents the market-clearing price and quantity.

Here is an example of a supply and demand graph for apples:

In this graph, S is the supply curve and D is the demand curve. The equilibrium point is where S and D cross, which shows that the market-clearing price for apples is $2 per kg and the market-clearing quantity is 10 kg.

The laws of supply and demand can help businesses make better decisions about their production, pricing, and marketing strategies. For example, if a business knows that the demand for its product is high and the supply is low, it can charge a higher price and increase its profits. On the other hand, if the demand for its product is low and the supply is high, it may need to lower its price or reduce its production to avoid losses.

However, the laws of supply and demand are not always fixed and can change due to various factors, such as:

- Changes in consumer preferences, tastes, income, or expectations

- Changes in production costs, technology, or efficiency

- Changes in government policies, taxes, subsidies, or regulations

- Changes in the availability of substitute or complementary goods or services

- Changes in weather, natural disasters, or other external shocks

These factors can cause shifts in the supply or demand curves, which can affect the equilibrium price and quantity. For example, if there is a drought that reduces the supply of apples, the supply curve will shift to the left, resulting in a higher equilibrium price and a lower equilibrium quantity. Conversely, if there is a new technology that increases the efficiency of apple production, the supply curve will shift to the right, resulting in a lower equilibrium price and a higher equilibrium quantity.

The degree to which changes in price affect the quantity demanded or supplied is called price elasticity. Goods or services that have high price elasticity are more responsive to changes in price, while goods or services that have low price elasticity are less responsive to changes in price. For example, luxury goods tend to have high price elasticity because consumers can easily switch to cheaper alternatives when their prices increase. On the other hand, necessities tend to have low price elasticity because consumers need them regardless of their prices.

Understanding the laws of supply and demand and their factors and effects can help businesses adapt to changing market conditions and optimize their performance. However, there are some limitations and assumptions of these laws that may not always hold true in reality. For example:

- The laws of supply and demand assume that markets are perfectly competitive, meaning that there are many buyers and sellers who have perfect information and no barriers to entry or exit. In reality, some markets may be dominated by a few large firms who have market power and can influence prices.

- The laws of supply and demand assume that consumers are rational and act in their own self-interest. In reality, some consumers may be influenced by emotions, biases, social norms, or other psychological factors that affect their choices.

- The laws of supply and demand assume that prices are flexible and adjust quickly to changes in supply or demand. In reality, some prices may be sticky or rigid due to contracts, regulations, menu costs, or other frictions that prevent them from changing.

Therefore, while the laws of supply and demand are useful tools for analyzing economic behavior and outcomes, they should not be taken as absolute truths but rather as simplified models that capture some aspects of reality.

FOREIGN TRADES

Foreign trade, refers to the exchange of capital, goods, and services across international borders or territories. It plays a significant role in most countries' economies, contributing to their gross domestic product (GDP). Foreign trade is similar to domestic trade, but it typically involves additional costs such as tariffs, border delays, and differences in language, legal systems, or culture. It encompasses imports (purchasing goods or services made in another country), exports (selling domestic-made goods in another country), and re-exports (importing goods from one country and re-exporting them to another).

The importance of foreign trade can be seen through various aspects:

Division of Labor and Specialization: Foreign trade leads to the division of labor and specialization at a global level. Countries specialize in producing and exporting goods that use abundant local resources while importing goods where resources are scarce.

Optimum Allocation and Utilization of Resources: Foreign trade allows countries to make the most efficient use of their resources by focusing on producing goods they have a comparative advantage in.

Equality of Prices: International trade helps equalize prices across countries by allowing consumers to access products from different regions.

Availability of Multiple Choices: Foreign trade provides consumers with a wider variety of goods and services that may not be available or more expensive to produce domestically.

Ensures Quality and Standard Goods: International competition encourages producers to maintain high-quality standards to remain competitive in the global market.

Raises Standard of Living: Foreign trade contributes to economic growth, job creation, and increased income levels, leading to an improved standard of living for people in participating countries.

Generate Employment Opportunities: International trade can create employment opportunities by stimulating economic activity across various sectors.

Facilitate Economic Development: Foreign trade can be a catalyst for economic development, particularly for developing countries seeking to integrate into the global economy.

Arbitrage trading involves taking advantage of price differences for the same asset in different markets. It requires at least two equivalent assets with differing prices. Arbitrage opportunities can arise between countries or even within small local towns within a specific country. By identifying these opportunities, traders can profit from the imbalance of asset prices.

Identifying arbitrage opportunities requires careful analysis and monitoring of market conditions. Traders often use news and other sources of information to identify special arbitrage trading opportunities[11]. Some common types of arbitrage include risk arbitrage (related to takeovers and mergers) and liquidation arbitrage. However, it's important to note that arbitrage trading involves risks and requires expertise in analyzing market conditions.

Example of intercity Arbitrage

Consider, for instance, the contrast between City A and City B where apples are priced at $3.50 and $1.50 per piece, respectively. When engaging in arbitrage business, it is always prudent to purchase low and vend high. Suppose you procure 20 apples from City B at a cost of $30 ($1.50 each) and then transport them to City A where they can be sold for $3.50 apiece; upon selling all 20 apples, your earnings will amount to $70 resulting in a profit of $40 after deducting the initial investment of $30.

It is important to note that this process may be repeated several times with a view toward establishing one's own system until the laws governing supply and demand come into play. Despite transportation expenses between cities, profits can still be realized even if walking or cycling rather than driving.

As an example of international arbitrage consider iPhones which sell for £1,199 in London: purchasing 50 such phones would entail an outlay of £59,950 (approximately equivalent to USD77k). In another country these same iPhones might sell for £1599 thereby generating total revenues of £79,950 (USD103k), yielding net profits of approximately USD26k after accounting for shipping costs as well as other associated fees - nonetheless remaining quite sizable overall!

AGAINST ALL ODDS

Perseverance, sacrifices, risk-taking, and working smart are all important factors that can contribute to success in business. Let's explore each of these aspects:

Perseverance: Perseverance is an essential quality for entrepreneurs. It allows you to keep going despite obstacles, difficulties, and setbacks. It gives you the strength and determination to stay motivated and focused on your goals.

Sacrifices: Success often requires sacrifices. Entrepreneurs may need to sacrifice their time, personal life, comfort, or financial stability to pursue their business goals. These sacrifices can be challenging but can also lead to long-term rewards.

Risk-taking: Taking calculated risks is a crucial part of entrepreneurship. Successful entrepreneurs understand that risks can lead to opportunities for growth and innovation. They carefully evaluate risks and make informed decisions to maximize their chances of success.

Working smart: Working smart involves finding efficient and effective ways to achieve your goals. It's about leveraging your resources, skills, and knowledge to optimize productivity and outcomes. Working smart allows entrepreneurs to achieve more with less effort.

By combining perseverance, sacrifices, risk-taking, and working smart, entrepreneurs increase their chances of overcoming challenges and achieving success in business. These qualities help them navigate the ups and downs of entrepreneurship and seize opportunities when they arise.

Remember that success in business is a journey that requires continuous learning, adaptation, and growth. Each entrepreneur's path may be unique, but these qualities can serve as guiding principles along the way.

Here is a success story of an entrepreneur that you might find inspiring:

Adi Dassler of Adidas: Adolf "Adi" Dassler, the founder of Adidas, started his shoemaking career in his mother's washroom in a small town in Bavaria, Germany. He was passionate about creating the best possible sports shoe for athletes. To stand out in the market, Dassler gathered feedback from athletes to understand their needs and preferences. This feedback allowed him to design athletic shoes that were highly valued by his customers.

In 1949, at the age of 49, Dassler registered "Adi Dassler Adidas Sportschuhfabrik" and introduced the first shoe with the iconic three stripes. His vision to create the best shoe for athletes was validated when the German national football team won the World Cup final in 1954 while wearing his new model of Adidas cleats. Since then, Adidas has grown into an international brand known for high-quality athletic wear.

Adi Dassler's story highlights the importance of listening to target customers and understanding their dreams, needs, and pain points. By focusing on customer value, he was able to create a product that resonated with athletes and built a successful brand.

Let me share with you a real-life story of Mr. Chitongwa, also known as Mr. Ten Kwacha, from Kamuswazi village in Zambia's Mbala district in the northern province. This account was related to me by my parents: Mrs. Mary Chisopa Sakala, the greatest businesswoman and hustler I have ever known who taught me the art of selling; and Mr. David Nkonde Sakala, an architectural engineer and soldier who served in the Zambian Air Force during President Kenneth Kaunda's reign in the 1970s until 2003 when he was transferred to Lusaka under President Levy

Patrick Mwanasa State Council—the third president after Frederick Titus Jacob Chiluba eventually my father retired from the zambia air force in 2009 whilst staying in ZAF Lusaka base.

During their stay in Mbala, my parents stumbled upon a great man's empire—Mr. Chitongwa—who was born in 1938 at Kamuswazi village of Mbala district where he grew up heading his father's cattle.

When he was seventeen years old (in 1955), he went to work for someone who paid him K10 (Ten Kwacha). Today this amount is equivalent to $0.48 but back then; it had much more value because Zambia's kwacha was one of Africa's strongest currencies.

Afterward, he left his village for Mbala town where he started buying sugar canes from Isoko and later sold them at Location Market using his K10 ($0.48) capital—a form of arbitrage trading we previously discussed under foreign trades if you've been following along nicely throughout this book.

After ten years repeating this process, he managed to raise approximately K200 ($9.54)—a considerable sum those days—with which he opened a shop named TEN KWACHA that eventually grew into a large establishment accompanied by a bar selling alcoholic beverages.

Over time through hard work on his farm along Mpulungu road rearing cattle, pigs, broiler chicken ,layers and goats while growing vegetables and Irish potatoes.

He bought a very big Mercedes Benz truck which he used to supply his Irish potatoes to the Copperbelt province and other parts of Zambia, coupled with consistent success led him to acquire many properties including beautiful cars and trucks making him Northern Province's richest man before representing Zambian farmers abroad someday

BECOMING A PRO OF THE GAME

To become a professional business person, there are several steps you can take:

1. Education: Acquire a solid foundation in business by pursuing relevant education. Consider obtaining a degree in business administration, finance, marketing, or a related field. Education provides valuable knowledge and skills that can help you navigate the business world.

2. Gain Experience: Gain practical experience by working in the business field. Look for internships, entry-level positions, or apprenticeships that allow you to learn from experienced professionals and develop your skills.

3. Continuous Learning: Stay updated with the latest trends, technologies, and best practices in your industry. Attend workshops, seminars, and conferences to expand your knowledge base and network with other professionals.

4. Networking: Build a strong professional network by connecting with like-minded individuals, industry experts, and potential mentors. Attend networking events, join professional associations, and engage in online communities to expand your network.

5. Develop Soft Skills: Cultivate essential soft skills such as communication, leadership, problem-solving, and adaptability. These skills are crucial for effective collaboration, decision-making, and managing relationships in the business world.

6. Embrace Challenges: Be open to taking on new challenges and responsibilities. Seek opportunities that allow you to grow both personally and professionally. Embracing challenges can help you develop resilience and adaptability.

7. Ethics and Integrity: Conduct yourself with integrity and adhere to ethical standards in all your business dealings. Building a reputation for trustworthiness and ethical behavior is essential for long-term success.

8. Seek Mentorship: Find a mentor who can provide guidance, support, and advice based on their experience in the business world. A mentor can offer valuable insights and help you navigate challenges along your career path.

Remember that becoming a professional business person is a continuous journey of learning and growth. Each person's path may vary, but these steps can serve as a foundation for success.

Here are some practical examples that highlight the qualities and actions that can make individuals stand out in the business industry:

1. Elon Musk: Elon Musk, the CEO of Tesla and SpaceX, is known for his visionary thinking and ability to disrupt traditional industries. His relentless pursuit of innovation and commitment to sustainable energy have made him a prominent figure in the business world.

2. Oprah Winfrey: Oprah Winfrey is a media mogul and philanthropist who built an empire through her talk show, magazine, and production company. Her authenticity, empathy, and dedication to empowering others have made her a highly influential businesswoman.

3. Jeff Bezos: Jeff Bezos, the founder of Amazon, is recognized for his customer-centric approach and focus on long-term growth. His relentless pursuit of excellence and willingness to take risks have contributed to Amazon's success as one of the world's largest e-commerce companies.

4. Mary Barra: Mary Barra, the CEO of General Motors, is known for her transformational leadership style and commitment to innovation. Under her leadership, General Motors has embraced electric vehicles and autonomous driving technologies, positioning the company for future success.

5. Warren Buffett: Warren Buffett, the chairman and CEO of Berkshire Hathaway, is widely regarded as one of the most successful investors in history. His disciplined investment approach, long-term perspective, and commitment to value investing have earned him a reputation as a business icon.

These individuals stand out in the business industry due to their unique qualities, innovative thinking, and ability to create lasting impact. While their paths to success may differ, they share common traits such as perseverance, adaptability, strategic thinking, and a focus on creating value for customers.

It's important to note that success in the business industry is not limited to these examples. There are countless other entrepreneurs and business leaders who have achieved remarkable success through their own unique journeys.

Remember that success in the business industry requires a combination of hard work, continuous learning, adaptability, and a passion for creating value. Each individual has their own path to success, so it's important to stay true to your own goals and aspirations.

HAVING MULTIPLE STREAMS OF INCOME

Dear youths please read in between the lines carefully.

Having multiple streams of income can provide financial security and flexibility. Here are some practical examples of different businesses that can generate multiple income streams:

1. Part-time Job: Taking on a part-time job in addition to your primary business can provide an extra source of income. It could be in the evenings, at night, or on weekends. A part-time job can help increase your living standards, savings ratio, or act as an emergency fund.

2. Freelancing Gigs: Freelancing tasks, such as web design or content writing, can be a way to utilize your expertise and earn additional income. Platforms like Fiverr and Upwork connect freelancers with clients seeking specific services.

3. Passive Income: Passive income refers to earnings generated with minimal effort or ongoing involvement. Examples include rental properties, investments, or online businesses. Platforms like eBay, Etsy, Gumroad, and Sellfy allow you to sell products online and generate passive income.

4. Affiliate Marketing: Affiliate marketing involves promoting products or services and earning a commission for each sale made through your referral. Programs like Google Adsense, Amazon Associates, and Share-a-Sale offer opportunities for affiliate marketing.

5. Teaching: Online teaching platforms like Udemy and Teachable enable you to create and sell courses on various topics. This can be a lucrative income stream if you have specialized knowledge or skills to share.

6. Subscription-based Services: Platforms like Patreon allow creators to offer exclusive content or perks to subscribers in exchange for recurring payments. This model works well for artists, writers, podcasters, and other content creators.

7. Consulting: If you have specialized knowledge or skills, offering consulting services can be a valuable income stream. You can provide consulting services in areas such as marketing, finance, human resources, or business strategy.

8. Real Estate: Investing in real estate properties for rental income or house flipping can generate substantial returns. This requires careful research and understanding of the real estate market.

9. Stock Market: Investing in stocks or other financial instruments can provide long-term capital appreciation and dividends. It's important to educate yourself about investing and seek professional advice if needed.

10. E-commerce: Starting an online store allows you to sell products directly to customers worldwide. Platforms like Shopify and WooCommerce provide tools to set up and manage your e-commerce business.

These are just a few examples of businesses that can generate multiple streams of income. The key is to identify opportunities that align with your skills, interests, and resources while diversifying your sources of revenue.

What I've outlined can help you generate money for the business of your dreams dear young man or woman. My fellow youths.

THE ART OF SELLING

Selling is an essential skill in business that requires tact, charisma, and effective communication. Here are some insights on mastering the art of selling:

1. Take an authoritative tone throughout the process: Sales is built on trust. Speaking with confidence and authority throughout the sales process helps establish yourself as a knowledgeable professional.

2. Develop and express your expertise: Showcase your knowledge and expertise to build credibility with potential customers. Demonstrate how your product or service can address their needs and provide value.

3. Sell with empathy and a personal touch: Understand your customers pain points and tailor your approach to address their specific needs. Show empathy and build a personal connection to establish trust.

4. Never stop learning and evolving as a salesperson: Stay updated with industry trends, customer preferences, and new sales techniques. Continuous learning helps you adapt to changing market dynamics and refine your sales strategies.

5. Manage your expectations: Set realistic goals and manage expectations throughout the sales process. Not every prospect will convert into a customer, but each interaction is an opportunity to learn and improve.

6. Employ the '1-10' sales closing technique: This technique involves asking prospects to rate their interest in your product or service on a scale of 1 to 10. Based on their response, you can tailor your approach to address any concerns or objections they may have.

Remember, selling is both an art and a skill that can be mastered with practice, experience, and continuous improvement. By combining these strategies with your unique strengths, you can enhance your sales effectiveness.

Selling and providing services are essential aspects of running a successful business. Here are some practical examples that entrepreneurs can consider to excel in these areas:

Selling:

Provide a solution to a problem: Understand your customers pain points and anticipate their needs. By offering products or services that address these challenges, you can capture their attention and build trust.

Develop expertise: Showcase your knowledge and expertise to build credibility with potential customers. Demonstrate how your product or service can add value and solve their problems just like I mentioned earlier on.

Sell with empathy: Show empathy towards your customers and understand their unique circumstances. Tailor your approach to address their specific needs and build long-term relationships.

Continuous learning: Stay updated with industry trends, customer preferences, and new sales techniques. Continuous learning helps you adapt to changing market dynamics and refine your sales strategies.

Utilize all available resources to continuously generate revenue. Consider selling a variety of products such as groceries, stationery, fruits, technology items, boutique goods, baked goods, artificial hair extensions, cosmetics and electronics. The key is to maintain a consistent flow of sales in whatever capacity possible.

Providing Services:

Identify service opportunities: Analyze the market and identify areas where you can provide valuable services. Look for gaps or unmet needs that align with your skills and expertise.

Deliver exceptional customer service: Focus on providing excellent customer service to differentiate yourself from competitors. Go the extra mile to exceed customer expectations and build long-term relationships.

Build a strong network: Networking is crucial for service-based businesses. Connect with industry professionals, potential clients, and mentors to expand your network and gain valuable insights.

Continuously improve: Seek feedback from clients and use it to improve your services. Embrace a growth mindset and be open to learning from both successes and failures.

Providing services is an incredibly reliable method to boost cash flow. If you possess skills such as document printing, photocopying, laminating, binding, and typing, consider offering these services specifically to students. Alternatively, if you are skilled in hair cutting or professional hair plaiting, opening a barber shop or salon respectively can be lucrative ventures - women especially love looking their best. Additional service offerings such as t-shirt printing and graphic design work can also bring in steady income streams. For those with videography or photography expertise, establishing a photo studio could prove profitable. Even small-scale jobs like car washing should not be overlooked; no job is too insignificant if it helps pay the bills (remember: pride does not pay bills). Those with culinary talents may find success by opening restaurants while others who offer lodging services should consider building guest houses or hotels for travelers and boarding houses for students. Finally, constructing rental properties such as houses and shops that provide monthly tenancy payments can generate substantial revenue streams over time. Offering internet access via an internet cafe is another viable business opportunity that shouldn't be dismissed lightly. The possibilities are endless - these examples merely scratch the surface of what one can do when providing exemplary services to others! Opening a radio station and TV station could be yet another platform to generate cash through advertisements.

Providing consultancy services for property and asset evaluations can result in substantial profits. Additionally, if you are adept at facilitating company and brand registrations on behalf of clients, assisting with passport applications or travel document processing, or securing international scholarships, there is potential for significant financial gain. Furthermore, establishing an agency that connects property and asset sellers with buyers while earning a commission from both parties is another lucrative opportunity to consider.

These are just a few examples of how entrepreneurs can excel in selling and providing services. Remember, success in business requires continuous learning, adaptability, and a customer-centric approach.

When selling and offering services be unique. Selling and offering services is the only way to make money in business.

THE UNTOLD TRUTH ABOUT BORROWING MONEY

Borrowing money can be a viable option for entrepreneurs, but it is important to understand the risks and benefits of taking on debt. Here are some facts that might help you make an informed decision:

When can you borrow money as an entrepreneur? : Entrepreneurs can borrow money at any stage of their business, but it is important to have a clear understanding of the purpose of the loan and how it will be repaid .

Why you shouldn't borrow money to start a business? :Borrowing money to start a business can be risky because it puts the entrepreneur in debt before they have generated any revenue. This can lead to financial stress and may even cause the business to fail

Why borrowing money is a danger to small businesses? :Borrowing money can be dangerous for small businesses because it increases their debt burden and interest payments. This can lead to cash flow problems and make it difficult for the business to grow.

How real estate tycoons leverage loans from private lenders and commercial banks to boost their business with practical examples? :Real estate tycoons often use loans from private lenders and commercial banks to finance their projects. These loans are secured by the property being developed, which reduces the risk for the lender. The tycoon then uses the loan proceeds to fund construction, marketing, and other expenses associated with the project. Once the project is completed, the property is sold or leased, and the loan is repaid with interest.

I hope this information helps you make an informed decision about borrowing money as an entrepreneur.

There are several alternative ways to finance a business, including:

1. Crowdfunding: This is a financing method that involves raising funds through the support of backers who typically contribute through an online platform. There are three types of crowdfunding: reward crowdfunding, debt crowdfunding, and equity crowdfunding . This one is highly appreciated In the Western world. Unlike in Africa.

2. Business credit cards: These are credit cards issued under the business's name and used solely for business purposes. Approval for a business credit card often depends on the business owner's personal credit and financial situation. Having a business credit card can help build business credit, offer rewards and bonuses, be useful in keeping personal and business expenses separate, and provide a relatively quick way to access cash.

3. Invoice financing: This is a financing method that involves selling unpaid invoices to a third-party company at a discount in exchange for immediate cash.

4. Merchant cash advances: This is a financing method that involves receiving an advance on future credit card sales. The lender will take a percentage of each sale until the advance is repaid with interest.

5. Venture capital: This is a type of private equity financing that involves investors providing capital to startups and small businesses in exchange for equity ownership .

6. Angel investors: These are wealthy individuals who provide capital to startups and small businesses in exchange for equity ownership.

7. Grants: These are non-repayable funds provided by governments, foundations, corporations, or other organizations to support specific projects or initiatives .

These are just some of the many alternative ways to finance a business. It is important to research each option carefully and choose the one that best fits your needs.

Now let's talk about the man who needs no introduction, Aliko Dangote. My role model.

Aliko Dangote, the richest person in Africa, began his business empire by borrowing **$3,000** from his uncle to import and sell agricultural commodities in Nigeria. Within three months of starting operations, he managed to repay the entire loan. This initial success laid the foundation for transforming his local commodities trading business into a multibillion-dollar corporation.

Today, Dangote Group, the conglomerate he founded more than three decades ago, is one of the largest private-sector employers in Nigeria and the most valuable conglomerate in West Africa. The group has interests in various industries such as cement production, sugar refining, flour milling, and petrochemicals. Dangote Cement, a subsidiary of Dangote Group, is the biggest producer of cement in Sub-Saharan Africa with operations in not less than 10 countries in Africa.

Dangote's entrepreneurial journey showcases his determination and business acumen. He started with a loan and transformed it into a thriving business empire that spans multiple industries and contributes significantly to Nigeria's economy

INDUSTRIALIZED ENTREPRENEURSHIP

Industrialized entrepreneurship has played a significant role in shaping economies and societies. Here are some more examples of industrialized entrepreneurship:

1. Benjamin Franklin: Known as America's original entrepreneur, Franklin's printing operations and publications, such as the Pennsylvania Gazette and Poor Richard's Almanack, were highly successful.

2. Henry Ford: Ford's mass production techniques and assembly lines revolutionized the automotive industry, making cars more affordable for millions of people.

3. John D. Rockefeller: Rockefeller was a key figure in the foundation of the oil industry. He founded Standard Oil, which became one of the world's first and largest multinational corporations.

4. Steve Jobs and Bill Gates :These tech pioneers transformed the ways humans connect and work through their hardware and software creations.

5. Oprah Winfrey: Winfrey's journey from poverty to international stardom is an inspiring example of entrepreneurial success.

6.Bonita Hair Salon and Blow Dry Bar: This Boston-based hair salon is an excellent example of small business entrepreneurship.

Industrialized entrepreneurship has played a significant role in shaping economies and societies. Here are some more examples of industrialized entrepreneurship:

These examples demonstrate how industrialized entrepreneurship has shaped various industries and impacted society. They highlight the importance of innovation, hard work, and strategic risk-taking in entrepreneurial endeavors . Industrialized entrepreneurship continues to drive economic growth and create change in the world.

Please note that these examples are just a few among many, and there are countless other entrepreneurs who have made significant contributions in their respective fields.

Elon Musk: Musk has played a pivotal role in the electric vehicle industry with Tesla, the aerospace industry with SpaceX, and the renewable energy industry with SolarCity (now part of Tesla)

Jeff Bezos: Bezos founded Amazon, which started as an online bookstore and has since expanded into various industries, including e-commerce, cloud computing, and digital streaming

7. Mark Zuckerberg: Zuckerberg co-founded Facebook, which has transformed the social media landscape and become one of the most influential companies in the technology industry .

8. Reed Hastings: Hastings co-founded Netflix, a streaming service that revolutionized the entertainment industry by offering on-demand access to movies and TV shows.

9. Travis Kalanick: Kalanick co-founded Uber, a ride-hailing platform that disrupted the transportation industry by providing an alternative to traditional taxis.

10. Brian Chesky: Chesky co-founded Airbnb, an online marketplace for short-term lodging that has transformed the hospitality industry.

11. Harry Oppenheimer was a South African mining magnate and businessman who played a significant role in the country's economic policies. He was the chairman of both Anglo-American Corporation and De Beers Consolidated Mines, which expanded their global reach and dominion. In South Africa, the Anglo powerhouse came to dominate the economy, which by the 1980s accounted for 25% of South Africa's GDP and an estimated 60% (or more) of the Johannesburg Stock Exchange.

These entrepreneurs have demonstrated the ability to identify gaps in existing industries and create innovative solutions to meet consumer needs. By doing so, they have not only built successful businesses but also shaped entire industries.

Renewable energy

The **renewable energy industry** focuses on the development and utilization of renewable energy technologies, which are derived from resources that can be naturally replenished within a human lifetime . These resources include sunlight, wind, water movement, and geothermal heat . The industry has experienced significant growth in recent years due to concerns about the environmental impacts of conventional fossil fuel sources, population growth, urbanization, and decreasing costs of renewable technologies.

Renewable energy has become an integral part of the global energy mix. In 2022, the worldwide renewable energy capacity reached **3,372 GW** . The consumption of renewable energy has also been on the rise, reaching **45.18 exajoules** in the same year . China has been a major contributor to renewable energy growth, followed by the United States, Japan, the United Kingdom, India, and Germany.

The renewable energy industry offers numerous benefits. It helps reduce greenhouse gas emissions and mitigate climate change by replacing fossil fuel-based energy sources with cleaner alternatives . It also contributes to energy security and decentralization by enabling distributed energy generation within the electric power distribution system . Furthermore, renewable energy can improve the quality of life and economic production while benefiting the environment.

By 2050, it is estimated that the renewable energy market will reach a value of **one trillion dollars**, equivalent to the current oil market size . This growth is driven by increasing global goals for net-zero emissions and the rising demand for solar and wind energy technologies.

COMMERCIAL FARMING AND LIVESTOCKS

Commercial farming refers to the large-scale production of crops and livestock for commercial purposes, such as selling in world markets or for profitable reasons. Livestock farming involves raising animals for various purposes, including meat, hides, wool, milk, and as work animals. Here are some practical examples of commercial farming and livestock:

1. Crops: Wheat, maize, coffee, sugarcane, tea, cashew, rubber, banana, and cotton are some examples of crops that are commercially farmed and harvested for sale in world markets .

2. Livestock: Cattle, pigs, sheep, goats, horses, mules, buffalo, and camels are commonly farmed for their meat, hides, wool, milk, and as work animals.

3. Dairy farming: Dairy farming involves rearing animals such as cows, buffaloes, camels and goats specifically for milk production. The milk is then used to produce dairy products on a large scale.

4. Fisheries: Commercial fisheries involve the cultivation of fish and other aquatic organisms for food or sale. Fish farms are established to rear fish in controlled environments.

These examples demonstrate the diverse range of commercial farming practices and the importance of agriculture in meeting global food demands. Commercial farming often utilizes modern technologies, machinery, and efficient irrigation methods to maximize productivity. It plays a crucial role in ensuring food security and supporting economic growth.

Please note that commercial farming practices may vary across regions and depend on factors such as climate conditions, market demand, and available resources.

I'm a farmer and I love this field so much such that I'll dedicate my time to write a book about commercial farming and livestock.

VALUE ADDITION

Value addition refers to the process of increasing the value of a product or service by adding features or enhancements that make it more appealing to customers. Here are some practical examples of value addition:

1. Sausages: Livestock farmers can add value to their meat by producing sausages. Sausages can be made from pork, beef, chicken, and other types of meat. This is a relatively simple business model that can help farmers increase their revenue.

2. Fruit and vegetable juices, blends, and smoothies: With more people becoming health-conscious, there is a growing demand for fruit and vegetable juices, blends, and smoothies. These products can be made from a variety of fruits and vegetables and offer a healthy alternative to sugary drinks.

3. Syrups: Syrups are thick liquids used as food toppings. They come in many different forms and flavors and can be used to enhance the taste of various foods.

4. Packaging: Packaging is an essential part of product marketing. By using attractive packaging designs, businesses can add value to their products and make them more appealing to customers.

5. Branding: Strong branding can add value to products or services by creating a positive image in the minds of customers. For example, Apple's logo is instantly recognizable and has become synonymous with quality and innovation.

6. Mealie meal: Mealie meal is a staple food in many African countries, including Zambia.

I'll talk about Zambia because I'm a Zambian. Value addition can be achieved by fortifying the mealie meal with essential vitamins and minerals such as iron, zinc, and vitamin A. This can help address malnutrition and improve the nutritional value of the food . Maize is processed into meal meal. An example of value addition. Which is sold in smaller quantities but at High prices.

7. Copper wires: Copper wires are used in various electrical applications, including power transmission and telecommunications. Value addition can be achieved by producing stranded copper wires, which are made by

twisting multiple thin copper wires together. Stranded copper wires are more flexible and durable than solid copper wires, making them ideal for use in high-stress applications . Zambia has been known to amongst the world's leading producers of copper.

These examples demonstrate how value addition can help improve the quality and appeal of products. By adding features or enhancements that meet customer needs, businesses can differentiate themselves from competitors and build brand loyalty.

Please note that these examples are just a few among many, and there are countless other ways to add value to products or services.

These examples demonstrate how value addition can help businesses increase their revenue and customer base. By adding features or enhancements that make their products more appealing, businesses can differentiate themselves from competitors and build brand loyalty.

INVESTING IN SHARES AND STOCKS

Investing in shares and stocks can be a great way to grow your wealth over time. Here are some key concepts and examples to help you get started:

What is investing? :Investing is the act of allocating resources, usually capital (i.e., money), with the expectation of generating an income, profit, or gains. It involves deploying capital toward projects or activities that are expected to generate a positive return over time.

What are stocks? :Stocks, also known as equities, represent ownership in a company. When you buy a stock, you become a shareholder in that company and have a claim on its assets and earnings.

How do stocks work? :Stocks are bought and sold on stock exchanges such as the New York Stock Exchange (NYSE) Lusaka stock exchange (LuSe) and NASDAQ. The price of a stock is determined by supply and demand in the market. If more people want to buy a stock than sell it, the price will go up, and vice versa.

How do you invest in stocks? :There are several ways to invest in stocks, including buying individual stocks, investing in mutual funds or exchange-traded funds (ETFs), or using robo-advisors . It's important to research each option carefully and choose the one that best fits your investment goals.

What are some examples of successful investors? : Some famous investors include Warren Buffett, Peter Lynch, Benjamin Graham, and Ray Dalio. These investors have achieved significant success by following their investment strategies and principles.

Investing in stocks can be a great way to build wealth over time. However, it's important to remember that investing involves risk and that past performance is not indicative of future results. It's important to do your research and consult with a financial advisor before making any investment decisions..

BUSINESS MARKETING

Certainly! Effective marketing and advertising skills are crucial for boosting your business, whether you choose to promote it traditionally or online. Here are some tips to help you get started:

1. Identify your target audience: Understand who your customers are, what they need, and how your product or service can meet those needs.

2. Create a marketing plan: Develop a comprehensive strategy that outlines your goals, target audience, key messages, and the channels you will use to reach your customers.

3. Build a strong brand: Establish a unique brand identity that reflects your business values and resonates with your target audience.

4. Leverage social media: Utilize popular social media platforms to engage with your customers, share valuable content, and build brand awareness.

5. Optimize your website: Ensure that your website is user-friendly, visually appealing, and optimized for search engines to improve its visibility online.

6. Invest in paid advertising: Consider running online ads on platforms like Google Ads or social media sites to reach a wider audience and drive traffic to your website.

7. Monitor and analyze results: Regularly track the performance of your marketing efforts, analyze data, and make adjustments as needed to optimize your campaigns.

Remember that effective marketing requires continuous learning and adaptation. Stay updated with the latest trends and techniques in the field to stay ahead of the competition.

EMPLOYEES MANAGEMENT

Managing employees effectively is a crucial aspect of running a successful business. Here are some tips to help you manage your employees both traditionally and online:

1. Find the right people for the job: Hiring the right people is essential to building a strong team. Look for candidates who have the necessary skills and experience, as well as a good cultural fit with your company.

2. Understand employee roles and responsibilities: Clearly define each employee's role and responsibilities to ensure that everyone knows what is expected of them.

3. Communicate effectively: Open communication is key to building trust and fostering a positive work environment. Encourage your employees to share their thoughts and ideas, and be receptive to feedback.

4. Provide feedback and recognition: Regularly provide feedback to your employees on their performance, both positive and negative. Recognize their achievements and contributions to the company.

5. Invest in employee development: Provide opportunities for your employees to learn new skills and grow professionally. This can include training programs, mentorship, or tuition reimbursement.

6. Create a positive work environment: Foster a positive work environment by promoting work-life balance, offering competitive compensation and benefits, and providing opportunities for social interaction among employees.

7. Stay up-to-date with employment laws: Keep up-to-date with employment laws and regulations to ensure that you are in compliance with all legal requirements.

Managing employees is an ongoing process that requires continuous learning and adaptation.

CIVIL SERVICE AND DOING BUSINESS

It is possible to launch a business while being a civil servant, although some restrictions may apply depending on the agency you work for . However, it is important to note that running a business while working in civil service can be challenging and requires careful planning and time management.

To run a successful business while working in civil service, you need to ensure that you have the necessary skills, resources, and support to manage both your job and your business. Here are some tips to help you get started:

1. Understand the rules: Before starting a business, make sure you understand the rules and regulations that apply to your situation. Some agencies may require you to obtain permission or disclose your business activities.

2. Develop a business plan: Create a comprehensive business plan that outlines your goals, target audience, key messages, and the channels you will use to reach your customers.

3. Manage your time effectively: Balancing work and business can be challenging, so it's important to manage your time effectively. Set clear priorities, delegate tasks when possible, and avoid overcommitting yourself.

4. Build a strong team: Surround yourself with a team of skilled professionals who can help you manage your business effectively.

5. Stay organized: Keep detailed records of your business activities, including finances, customer interactions, and marketing efforts.

6. Stay up-to-date with industry trends: Stay informed about the latest trends and developments in your industry to stay ahead of the competition. If you've noticed I've made several emphasis on this.

HOW TO SELL ANYTHING

Knowing how to sell anything is an important skill that can help you succeed in any role that requires the promotion of ideas or products. Here are some tips to help you get started:

1. Research your buyer: It's important to know who you're selling to because it helps you communicate effectively to your customer, which can then lead to more sales. When you understand your customers, it can be easier to give them what they need. Research your target customer or target persona to learn more about their needs, wants, lifestyle, motivations and perspective. From there, you can adapt your sales pitch accordingly.

2. Learn about your customer's needs: When you sell a product or service, you're often selling a solution. Try to find out what problem your product can solve or what desire it can fulfill. There are many tools available to help you research potential needs and problems affecting customers, including web analytics, social media tools or data from your competitors.

3. Know what your product or service offers: Understand the benefits of your product or service and how it can help your customers. Be prepared to articulate these benefits clearly and concisely.

4. Sell yourself: Establishing a personal connection with your customers can help build trust and rapport. Be confident, enthusiastic, and passionate about what you're selling.

5. Establish a rapport before selling: Building a relationship with your customers before trying to sell them something can help increase the chances of success. Take the time to get to know them and their needs.

6. Present yourself as an expert: Position yourself as an authority in your field by sharing valuable insights and information with your customers.

7. Listen actively: Listening carefully to your customers can help you understand their needs and concerns better. This can help you tailor your sales pitch accordingly.

8. Offer customer service: Providing excellent customer service can help build loyalty and repeat business. Be responsive, helpful, and attentive to your customers' needs.

BECOME A BUSINESS TYCOON

Becoming a business tycoon requires a combination of skills, knowledge, and experience. Here are some tips to help you get started:

1. Be creative: Always be looking for ways to improve your business and to make it stand out from the competition. Recognize that you don't know everything and be open to new ideas and new approaches to your business.

2. Get organized: Organization will help you complete tasks and stay on top of things to be done. A good way to do this is to create a to-do list each day – as you complete each item, check it off your list. This will ensure that you're not forgetting anything and you're completing all the tasks that are essential to the survival of your business.

3. Be consistent: Consistency is a key component to making money in business. You have to consistently keep doing the things necessary to be successful day in and day out. This will create long-term positive habits that will help you make money over the long term.

4. Analyze your competition: Competition breeds the best results. To be successful, you can't be afraid to study and learn from your competitors. After all, they may be doing something right that you can implement in your business to make more money.

5. Understand the risks and rewards: The key to being successful is taking calculated risks to help your business grow. A good question to ask is "What's the downside?"

6. Concentrate on objectives: Successful people maintain focus on their objectives and prioritize their time accordingly.

7. Lead: Leadership is a skill that can be learned, developed, and improved over time. Effective leaders inspire their employees, communicate a clear vision, and make decisions that benefit the company as a whole.

8. Make quick and accurate decisions: Successful entrepreneurs are able to make quick decisions using available data while also considering the potential risks and rewards.

9. Accept sacrifices for the business: Running a successful business requires hard work, dedication, and sacrifice. Be prepared to put in long hours and make personal sacrifices for the sake of your business.

10. Provide excellent service: Providing excellent customer service can help build loyalty and repeat business. Be responsive, helpful, and attentive to your customers' needs.

SHOULD FAILURE STOP YOU?

Anyone can fail but failure shouldn't put and end to your dreams. Try and fail but never fail to try. Listen to me it's okay to try again and again and again. Let me share with you this incredible story of jack ma.

Jack Ma, the founder of Alibaba Group, is a well-known entrepreneur who has faced many failures in his life before achieving success. He failed primary school twice and middle school three times. He also failed his university entry exam three times. He was rejected by the police force and even KFC. He applied for Harvard ten times and was rejected each time.

Despite these setbacks, Jack Ma persevered and eventually founded Alibaba Group in 1999 with 18 others, working out of an apartment in Hangzhou. Today, Alibaba is one of the largest commercial networks in the world . Jack Ma's story is a testament to the power of perseverance and determination.

So had jack ma stopped by so much failures we couldn't have known about the multi billion dollars Alibaba Group today.

Keep trying, keep pushing you never know something big can happen to you and you can also have a story to share.

ACCESSING THE MILLIONAIRE'S LEAGUE

Earning a million dollars is not easy, but it is possible. Here are some ways to earn your first million:

1. Invest in real estate: Real estate is one of the most lucrative ways to earn a million dollars. You don't need special qualifications to become a real estate investor. As long as you have the money to buy a property, you can invest in real estate. You can also consider investing in real estate investment trusts (REITs) or real estate crowd funding platforms.

2. Start a business: Starting a business can be another way to earn a million dollars. You can start a business in any industry that you're passionate about and that has the potential for growth. However, starting a business requires careful planning, hard work, and dedication.

3. Purchase cheap stocks: Investing in stocks can be another way to earn a million dollars. You can purchase cheap stocks that have the potential for growth and hold onto them for the long term.

4. Start a side hustle: A side hustle is another way to earn extra income. You can start a side hustle in your free time and gradually grow it into a full-time business.

5. Protect your wealth: Once you've earned your first million dollars, it's important to protect your wealth by investing in diversified assets, such as stocks, bonds, and real estate.

Remember that earning a million dollars requires hard work, dedication, and careful planning. Stay updated with the latest trends and techniques in the field to stay ahead of the competition.

Investing in the milling industry, both maize and wheat processing, is a wise decision. Maize is a versatile multi-purpose crop that is primarily used as feed globally, but also important as a food crop, especially in sub-Saharan Africa and Latin America, besides other non-food uses. Global maize production has surged in the past few decades, propelled by rising demand and a combination of technological advances, yield increases and area expansion. Wheat, maize and rice are the world's leading staple cereals.

Also investing in soya beans cultivation Soya beans is a species of legume native to East Asia, widely grown for its edible bean, which has numerous uses. Soybeans are an important component of Asian diets and have been consumed for thousands of years. Today, they are mainly grown in Asia and South and North America. In Asia, soybeans are often eaten whole, but heavily processed soy products are much more common in Western countries. Various soy products are available, including soy flour, soy protein, tofu, soy milk, soy sauce, and soybean oil.

Investing in soya beans can be a good decision as they are a versatile crop with numerous uses. They can be used to produce various food products such as tofu and soy milk. Soybean oil is also used in cooking and industrial applications .

Cooking oil processing is another industry worth investing in. Many cooking oils are extracted from seeds, nuts or fruits. They are typically either expeller pressed or extracted using chemicals. Once extracted, oils can be refined to change the appearance, taste, smell and more .

Petroleum refining is also a lucrative industry to invest in. Petroleum refining or oil refining is an automated procedure that removes crude oil from the earth and converts it into usable items such as liquefied petroleum gas (LPG), kerosene, asphalt foundation, jet fuel, diesel, heating oil, cooking oils, etc.

Mining is another industry that can be profitable. Mining is required to obtain most materials that cannot be grown through agricultural processes or feasibly created artificially in a laboratory or factory. Ores recovered by mining include metals, coal, oil shale, gemstones, limestone, chalk, dimension stone, rock salt, potash, gravel and clay.

Large scale commercial farming and livestock are also good investment options. The grain milling sector plays a vital role in food security as its products are the primary ingredients of staple foods.

Financial services are an essential part of any economy. They provide services such as banking and insurance to individuals and businesses. You can also provide loans to civil servants and collateral based loans to people in the private sector.

The food industry is another sector worth investing in. The extraordinary growth in the traditional and new markets and evolving new consumer trends present operators in the maize industry with opportunities and challenges.

Information technology is another lucrative industry to invest in. It includes computer hardware and software development as well as internet-based services.

The automotive industry is another sector worth investing in. It includes the design, development, production and sale of motor vehicles.

The energy industry includes companies involved in the production and sale of energy such as oil companies and power utilities.

The jewelry industry involves the design, manufacture and sale of jewelry items such as rings, necklaces and bracelets .

Drugs (biotechnology) involve the use of living organisms to develop new drugs for treating diseases.

Electrical equipment involves the design and manufacture of electrical equipment such as transformers and generators.

Healthcare products include medical devices such as surgical instruments and diagnostic equipment.

The transportation industry is a lucrative multi-million dollar sector. Consider investing in this field by starting with a taxi business and upgrading to small or large-scale operations for local, intercity, and international travel. Moreover, you can explore opportunities as a transporter of various goods and commodities to earn profits from your transport services. Begin with a modest truck and progress towards larger vehicles or even own an airline since transportation involves the movement of people or goods between different locations.

E-commerce involves buying and selling goods over the internet.

Software engineering firms develop software applications for businesses or consumers .

Electronics general dealing involves buying and selling electronic goods such as televisions and computers.

When trying to earn a million dollars, there are several common mistakes that you should avoid:

1. Not having a plan: Having a plan is essential to achieving your financial goals. Without a plan, you may not know what steps to take to reach your goal of earning a million dollars.

2. Not investing wisely: Investing wisely is crucial to building wealth. Avoid investing in high-risk investments that promise quick returns, as these are often scams.

3. Spending too much money: Spending too much money can quickly deplete your savings and make it difficult to achieve your financial goals. Avoid overspending on unnecessary items and focus on saving and investing your money instead.

4. Not diversifying your investments: Diversifying your investments is important to minimize risk and maximize returns. Avoid putting all your money into one investment or asset class.

5. Not seeking professional advice: Seeking professional advice from a financial advisor or accountant can help you make informed decisions about your finances and avoid costly mistakes.

CONCLUSION

Dear reader,

At this moment allow me address you as a Chief Executive Officer CEO of your own brands. I'm confident beyond reasonable doubt that you have grasped each concept outlined in my book.

Allow me to present the final principles that I have gleaned from experts in reverse psychology, which you should make sure to comprehend fully. Reverse psychology is a tactic used to obtain what you desire by requesting or implying the opposite of what it is you truly want. This method of manipulation encourages the target to act contrary to expectations.

The following are the guidelines:

1. Purchase when others are selling. Wait for sellers to deplete their stock; they will ultimately become buyers, leaving you as the sole seller in your specific market. Sell when everyone else is buying, but only at higher prices due to scarcity and demand conditions within the market.

2. Do not invest or start a business during an optimistic period; instead, wait for a bearish market during times of recession and poor economic conditions when rivals are weak so that you can hire employees and buy materials cheaply.

3. Avoid chasing money; rather, establish a business because money does not create businesses - businesses produce wealth.

4. Instead of relying on paychecks from employers, concentrate on earning income outside traditional employment arrangements since regular paydays cultivate slave mentalities rather than mastermind ones.

5. Take risks because failure entails valuable lessons while success results in extravagant riches

6. If your country's economy seems too strong, begin your enterprise elsewhere before returning once it has gained momentum and your national economy collapses- this way you will be stronger upon re-entry into your homeland

7. Understand that reality is fake while fakeness constitutes true reality in reverse psychology. The financial system must be manipulated but only after comprehending its workings.

In conclusion, money creation should serve one purpose: elevating oneself above all other entities. Once having achieved wealth status, no longer would one need work under systems, but those systems would function according to one's wishes thereby rendering them tools for personal gain

Dear Reader,

I hope this book has been an eye-opener for you, and that it has inspired you to think differently about money. The title of this book, "Money Can Be Created," is not just a catchy phrase, but a powerful statement that reflects the core message of this book.

The truth is, money is not something that is created by a select few. It is something that can be created by anyone who has the right mindset and the right tools. This book provides you with those tools, and I hope it has given you the inspiration and motivation you need to take control of your financial future.

Remember, creating wealth is not just about making more money. It's about creating a life of abundance and freedom, where you have the resources to pursue your dreams and live life on your own terms. I hope this book has helped you take the first step towards that life.

Thank you for reading "Money Can Be Created." I wish you all the best on your journey towards financial freedom.

Sincerely,

ROY SAKALA.

References

1. Forbes marketing strategies & successful business stories.

2. Investopedia, Assets and liabilities. Real estate.

3. Reverse psychology, power principals and arbitrage.

4. Encyclopedic laws of supply and demand.

5. Sir Francis bacon 1597.

Author contact details

Email: roysakala5@gmail.com

Phone: +260970305016 also used on WhatsApp.

Facebook: https://www.facebook.com/roysakalaofficial

For mentorships and book procurement services, contact the author.